'The Natural Storyteller is testament to the grace, mystery and joy that have shaped human relationships with the earth and its abundant expression. natural way for people to be, and be well. The stories in Georgia lection welcome us back into that special space and place, in whiwe truly belong.'

T0294134

Dr Donald Smith, Directo

'To protect our planet, in this hour of chronic need, we have to completely re-imagine our relationship with the natural world and all its wondrous diversity. Storytelling plays a crucial part in that healing process, especially (but not only!) for young people, as Georgiana Keable so beautifully and powerfully reveals in The Natural Storyteller.'

Jonathon Porritt CBE, Forum for the Future

'On a cold winter's night last December, I was pulled hesitantly onto a stage, before I found myself running out into the world through Georgiana's storytelling. My companions, world-leading climate scientists, swiftly followed. There is something so wonderfully comforting about listening to a story – a pleasure that many of us have forgotten since our youth. Comforting and challenging – stories have so much to say to us, if we would but listen. In an increasingly fragmented world, suffering the impacts of climate change, stories bridge divides and bring us back together. Let Georgiana's stories open your eyes and ears once more. Let Georgiana's inspiration become your inspiration piece. Now more than ever, we all need to become storytellers. In Georgiana's words, "See the story and it will live through you and your body – naturally." A glorious anthology that grounds our feet in the roots of the earth and opens our hearts to each other.'

Professor Ros Cornforth, meteorologist and Director of
The Walker Insitute for Climate System Research

'A life of dedication to nature, storytelling and young people courses through the pages of The Natural Storyteller. It is written with intimacy, information and chock full of good stories and creative reflective activities. It is a wonderful and needed resource for children in today's world.'

Laura Simms, storyteller and author

'I think The Natural Storyteller is a brilliant book for young people, but it doesn't end there. Anyone interested in storytelling as an art form, but doesn't know how to get started, would find this an excellent place to begin. I can very much recommend it for anyone starting down the Bard path, and anyone interested in finding emotionally sustainable approaches to activism. It's an uplifting read that will leave you with a sense of possibility and optimism — something I think we could all do with right now.'

Nimue Brown, Spiral Nature Magazine

The Natural Storyteller is a gorgeous heart-warming book full of stories that children (and people any age!) can relate to. It is a collection of stories, carefully gathered over a period of years, from all over the world. What steals my heart about this book is that it unflinchingly addresses the turmoil and realities of life in the 21st century. The author does not shy away from tackling themes such as deforestation, war or corporate greed. This book is that rare thing: it unlocks emotions, ideas and a wild surge of creativity.

Imelda Almqvist, Paganpages

'Storytelling is one of those things that I struggle with but also see how powerful it can be in engaging kids and adults. Your book has really opened my eyes and given me the confidence to get out there and do it!

Mark Lloyd, Forest School teacher

The Natural Storyteller
Wildlife Tales for Telling

Georgiana Keable

Hawthorn Press

The Natural Storyteller © 2017 Georgiana Keable

Georgiana Keable is hereby identified as the author of this work in accordance with section 77 of the Copyright, Designs and Patent Act, 1988. She asserts and gives notice of her moral right under this Act.

Hawthorn Press

Published by Hawthorn Press, Hawthorn House,
1 Lansdown Lane, Stroud, Gloucestershire, GL5 1BJ, UK
Tel: (01453) 757040   Email: info@hawthornpress.com
www.hawthornpress.com

Cover image © Shirin Adl
Cover and book design by Lucy Guenot
Typeset in Scala and Jacqueline
Storymaps by Georgiana Keable
Printed by Henry Ling Ltd, The Dorset Press, UK 2017, 2019

Every effort has been made to trace the ownership of all copyrighted material. If any omission has been made, please bring this to the publisher's attention so that proper acknowledgement may be given in future editions.

The views expressed in this book are not necessarily those of the publisher.

Printed on environmentally friendly chlorine-free paper sourced from renewable forest stock.

British Library Cataloguing in Publication Data applied for

ISBN 978-1-907359-80-4

To my favourite storytellers – Mum and Dad

Contents

Introduction

The Natural Storyteller – Is You!

This book is like a packet full of seeds. When you open the book and read a story seed, you plant it in yourself. The more you water this story seed the bigger it will grow. You may find yourself growing into a *Natural Storyteller*.

Maybe you don't want to tell stories. That's totally fine! Just enjoy the book. However, here are some reasons why you might consider being a storyteller:

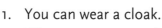

1. You can wear a cloak.
2. When you are stranded on Mars, or in a lift that got stuck and you have no mobile phone or book, you can still enjoy loads of stories in your mind.
3. Your life is your own story. Telling stories can give you clues about how you want your story to grow. You will be able to explain all kinds of things in an interesting story kind of way.
4. Stories can be medicine. And being a storyteller can be true fun.

What kind of stories are in this book?

Here you will find myths, legends and fairytales. You will find tales of real life. You will find histories of people who were seriously brave. You will find stories of talented sparrows, enchanted trees and superhuman deer.

Every story in this seed-packet-book is about that outlandish-beyond-astounding-and-staggering stuff we call nature. That weird and incredible more-than-human world.

These stories come from peoples all over the world who live close to each other and to nature. People who see that nature's wild beings are often great travellers. A cuckoo flies from England way over the Sahara Desert to Africa and a salmon swims from America to the Arctic. And the stories themselves have travelled, without passports, flying over many borders to land in this book.

Adventure stories

In Norway, where I live, the word for 'story' is the same as the word for 'adventure'. This book is about having adventures. As you read it you may find your family gets bigger, you may become a tracker for wild cousins, you may discover you have relatives with extremely long roots and you might get the urge to go on a quest to save a squirrel. I'm not promising anything but you never know.

Story Heart

If the world was utterly jolly and happy all the time there would be no stories and it might be rather a boring place to live. However, there are lots of quests, disasters and excitements to keep us awake and on our toes. Heroes and heroines who are navigating dangerous waters need a good heart. That is usually more important to them than big muscles, a hairy chest or frilly clothes. They need to be brave and think with their heart.

Where do daring heroines and heroes keep their *Story Heart*? Same place as you keep your heart – in a cage, your ribcage, which protects it as it beats every moment of every day. Maybe you feel it – 'Dunk, dunk, dunk!'

This first chapter starts with a riddle:

You talk to me, but I have no words,

You sing to me, but I play no music,

You love me, though I am a stranger.

Who am I?

If you haven't worked out this riddle by the end of *Story Heart*, you will find the answer there. Meanwhile listen to the secrets hidden in the ribcage.

The Story of Tasoo

Long ago, a tiny bird flew through an enormous forest. The little bird's name was Tasoo. As he flew his bright eyes saw monkeys jumping in the trees and his little ears heard butterflies on the wing.

In the sky above Tasoo the sun was blazing down fiery and hot. Below him on the forest floor the dry grass was beginning to smoulder. Wind blew onto the grass and soon the glowing grasses burst into fire. Before long the whole forest was ablaze. All the animals from the largest elephant to the tiniest mouse ran and galloped away to save their skins. Above them the birds soared high into the air to save their feathers.

All except Tasoo. His little eyes went red with determination and he flew down through the flames to the river. Filling his tiny beak with water, he flew, back and forth, back and forth, and drops of water dripped onto the roaring furnace. On and on he flew, until his tiny wings were burnt and singed again and again. It seemed impossible that he had the strength to keep flying, yet he did.

High above, sitting on their silver clouds, all the gods peered down on him. Rubbing their eyes in disbelief, they saw this tiny heart of courage. Drop by drop all the gods began to cry. From their tears the rain poured as if gigantic buckets were being emptied down onto the forest and the fire was quenched.

Little Tasoo sat on a branch, dripping wet. Around him the animals and birds returned to the forest. Tasoo felt so happy he did what birds do. He began to sing.

When you feel like telling a story make sure it's one you really like. It's good to start with a really short one like Tasoo. To help remember it you can make a map of the story – like this ...

True or False?

To help remember this story, say if the following are true or false:

1. Tasoo was a monkey.
2. The sun was blazing down on the forest.
3. All the animals ran for their lives.
4. The gods were busy playing computer games so they did not notice the forest burning.
5. Tasoo celebrated in typical bird style, with a good old sing-song.

Myths from the Land of You

Have you ever seen or been someone brave? Not necessarily a megabrave superhero like Tasoo or Spiderman. Sometimes a little thing like giving someone a look when they are being mean can take a lot of courage. What happened? This is the stuff that stories are made of.

Wangari and the Green Belt

Do you know how big Africa is? It is so enormous that the whole of India could fit in it, the whole of China, plus the whole of North America and most of Europe.

Over a hundred and thirty years ago the powerful European countries took a map of Africa, cut it up and shared it out as if it was an enormous pizza. France, you take this slice. Germany, you can have that bit, Britain, this. Do you think they asked the African people? No.

Britain was given a huge and beautiful country called Kenya.

There in Kenya in 1930, a child was born. An ordinary African child, born in a round house made of earth. As soon as she was born three women came in with gifts. One woman was carrying a sweet potato, the second brought blue sugar cane, the third brought sweetcorn. The new mother took juice from all these and dripped it into the mouth of the newborn baby. So the first thing the baby tasted was not mother's milk, but the fruits of the earth. The baby was given the name of an African goddess – Wangari.

Wangari's dad was tall and clever. He was a car mechanic. He was so strong that if he needed to change the wheel on a car he just lifted up the whole car, took out the old wheel and slung in a new one. Wangari's mum was also tall and her whole life no one ever heard her say an angry word.

Wangari had one dad and four mothers. She called them Big Mummy, Mummy (her real birth mother), Little Mummy and Younger Mummy. How can you have four mothers? At that time in Kenya a man who was rich enough could marry several women, as long as he promised to look after all his children. So Wangari had lots of sisters and brothers to play with.

When she was seven years old her dad said, 'Wangari, your mother and I want your brothers to go to school and there is no school here. You will go with your mother to your grandparents' village. I will not be there, so she will need your help.'

When they got to her new village Wangari stared wide-eyed. All around the village was the most beautiful forest she had ever seen. Her grandmother hugged her and said, 'Wangari, go out and play in the rain, then you will grow as tall as the trees.'

Wangari was only seven years old but she worked hard. She planted seeds, looked after her younger sister and brother, washed clothes and made food. She fetched firewood but her mum said she should never take wood from the fig tree, which was God's tree. She promised, but she often played beside it because there was the fresh water bubbling up and little frogs hopping around.

One day, as she was serving a dish of steaming ugali porridge to her big brother, he said, 'Mum, why doesn't Wangari go to school?'

'Now that's a good question, my son!' said her mum and, sure enough, soon Wangari became the first girl in the family to go to school.

On her very first school day Wangari's cousin walked with her. 'Can you read and write, Wangari?' he asked.

'No, I can't,' she said.

He proudly took out a pencil and wrote a big W on his book, then he took out a rubber and rubbed it out. 'Wow, that's magic!' Wangari wanted to learn this magic.

Wangari stayed at school and over the years worked very hard. On her last day she was amazed. She had won the prize as the cleverest pupil in the whole school!

Her mum said, 'Wangari, we have decided that you will go on to the high school. It's far away. Be brave – we love you.'

So Wangari set off alone. Her sack was light, for she had only one dress to carry, a present from her brother. She had no shoes – she didn't get those until she was fifteen.

The new school was run by nuns. Many of the nuns had come from Europe and Wangari thought they were kind to leave their homes and help girls in Kenya. However some of the nuns were very strict. The girls were never allowed to speak their own language – their mother tongue. If they did they had to wear a badge which said, 'I am stupid, I spoke my mother tongue today.' Wangari worried that she would not understand her grandmother when she went home, but luckily she still dreamed in her own language.

At this time a terrible war began. Over the years not only had their country been taken over but so many unfair things had happened. Kenyan men fought bravely for Britain in the Second World War. But when they came home their farms had been given away to British soldiers! Their country had been taken away and now even their farms. This was the final straw and Kenyans began to fight to get their own country back.

At her school Wangari was sheltered from violence and the girls were told that the African fighters were wrong. Wangari loved learning and when the last day of school came she was amazed.

'Wangari,' said her friends, 'you have won the prize as the cleverest girl in the whole school! You could be a nurse, or even a teacher. What will you be?'

'Neither,' said Wangari. 'I want to go on studying. I want to learn everything there is to know about nature – forests, animals and birds!'

'What?' said her friends. 'Don't be ridiculous, Wangari, you are not a man.'

But Wangari's dream came true. Along with other bright Kenyan students she got a scholarship from the president of America. For five-and-a-half years she studied biology in America. After all that time, you can imagine how excited she was on the long boat ride home over the ocean.

At last, nearing the coastline, she saw a big group of people singing and as she drew nearer she could see it was her family. Big Mummy, Mummy, Little Mummy, Younger Mummy, Dad, Grandmother, all the sisters and brothers, singing for her! As she ran down the gangplank she was crying with happiness.

Her aunty stared at her and said, 'Wangari, what is wrong, you are so thin! Don't they have proper food in America? Why have they been starving you?'

Wangari laughed. 'Don't you know it's fashionable in America to be skinny and thin, not like Kenya where it's beautiful to be big and gorgeous. I'm so happy to be home!'

Kenya was now an independent country. Wangari got a job at the university and she kept studying nature. She became a professor; in fact she was the first woman professor in the whole of Central and East Africa. By this time she had saved enough money to buy herself a car. There were not many women in Kenya who had their own car and she was excited to drive out to the village where her grandparents lived.

Even before she had arrived she stopped the car. She was confused, staring at the landscape that she knew so well. How could it be? The great beautiful green forest was gone. Instead she saw mile upon mile of tea and coffee bushes.

Her heart pounding, she approached her family house and saw a beloved figure sitting outside. 'Grandmother,' she called, 'where is the forest? What happened?'

'Money, my child,' said her grandmother. 'They have cut the forest for money. But they have forgotten that money cannot buy everything. Money is no home to the birds of the forest, for mother elephant and brother monkey. Money cannot shade us from the hot sun. Money cannot be burned on our cooking fire. Money will not stop the earth from washing away in the floods or bring sweet rain for our crops.'

Water! The land was so dry. Wangari ran to the fig tree where she used to play, God's tree. Where it had stood was a dried old stump and the clear delicious water and the little frogs were gone too. Wangari knew now from her studies that the fig tree has a root that goes so deep it always finds water. The tree was gone and the land was dry. She looked around at the children of the village and saw many who looked hungry and unwell. 'Yes, child,' said her grandmother. 'People use the money from coffee to buy white bread and sweets for their children. They no longer grow good vegetables and they can no longer pick the fruits and nuts of the forest, which used to be free.'

Wangari was so angry. She got into her car and drove straight back into the city, straight to the government building, and took the lift up to the forestry department.

'I want to plant trees. No, I am going to plant a forest!' she said to the forestry minister.

'Well, Professor Wangari, I know you are very clever, but how can you plant a whole forest?'

'It's simple,' she said. 'The people of Kenya will help me.' Wangari wrote in the newspapers, she spoke on the radio and to crowds of people, saying, 'Cutting down our forest is destroying our beautiful Kenya. It's making our children hungry and our animals and birds are losing their homes. There is a simple solution. We will plant trees!'

Sure enough, women and men listened to her words. Little by little they learnt to scarify, soak, stratify and plant tree seeds. They cared for the tiny saplings so that no one trod on them and no stray goat ate them. A great new forest grew up. Wangari and her friends called this work the Green Belt movement because they were planting long green belts of forest over the whole of Kenya.

Meanwhile Wangari was also determined to protect the old forest that remained. When she heard that an ancient forest was in danger she went with groups of students. They stood bravely before the bulldozers and the chainsaws. The rich people who owned these forests were furious. They made up lies about her in the newspapers, they threatened her and at last they sent her to prison. Many times she was locked up in prison for protecting forests and people.

Do you think Wangari gave up? No! One day she got a letter in the post. It was from Norway. She had won perhaps the highest honour a person can receive in this world. She had been given the Nobel Peace Prize. She and the thousands of women and men who had helped her were so proud. And they kept planting trees.

Wangari was a real person, a warm and inspiring person whom I was lucky enough to meet. When she came to Norway for the Nobel Peace Prize a group of African women asked me to come and tell her a story. She was the best listener – you could see from the expressions on her face that she was listening to every word. Maybe that's what made her brave; she listened to what people and trees needed.

Here is the Wangari Maathai Quiz, to help remember her story:
1. How many mums did Wangari have?
2. What was so special about 'God's tree'?
3. Where did Wangari study?
4. Why did the Kenyan people get angry?
5. What was happening to the forest?
6. Why did Wangari go to prison?
7. What was the prize she got?

This next story is about John who had a big heart and tried not to listen to it.

The Pedlar of Swaffham

In a town called Swaffham in England lived a man named John. His house was so small that he could sit on his chair and shut the front door with his right hand and the back door with his left hand and warm his hands on the fire without moving. In his tiny garden grew an apple tree. In the spring the tree was white with blossom and in the summer it was red with apples.

John lived around six hundred years ago when there were few shops and nobody had a car. John walked around with a big sack filled with buttons, ribbons, knives and other things to sell. Though John had a small house he had a big heart, and when he was out selling his wares he might see an old widow who needed a knife, or a boy with sparkling eyes gazing at a football, or a young lady taking some bright buttons in her hand. John couldn't help himself. He gave away more than he sold. And so the day came, as it had to, when there was nothing left in his sack.

That day, John looked in his pockets, but they were completely empty. He searched in his cupboards. They were empty too. In the garden the apples were long gone from the old apple tree. That night John went to bed hungry and, as hungry people often do, he had a dream.

In his dream the door opened and a man in shining white clothes appeared, calling, 'John! Wake up! Go down to London and stand on London Bridge. There you will hear something to your advantage.'

That morning John woke up with a start and thought, 'Ho, what a good dream, but after all it was only a dream.'

That day he dug over his little potato patch and found two tiny potatoes. But two small tatties don't fill an empty stomach, so that night he went to bed hungry and, as hungry people often do, he had a dream ...

Once again the door opened and the man in shining white clothes said, 'Wake up, John! Go to London town and stand on London Bridge, where you will hear something to your advantage.'

'What? The same dream again? But it's only a daft dream.' So John scoured his cupboards and right at the back he found a few tea leaves. But a cup of tea doesn't fill an empty stomach and oh that night he was hungry. His belly was aching and he was twisting and turning in his bed. At last he fell asleep and as hungry people will do he had a dream ...

This time there was a hammering and a thundering on the door and the man came bursting in, with his shining white clothes and shouting, 'JOHN! WAKE UP! GO TO LONDON TOWN AND STAND ON LONDON BRIDGE AND YOU WILL HEAR SOMETHING GOOD. AND I'M NOT TELLING YOU AGAIN!!'

What could he do? Was he a foolish dreamer? He was sure that London was full of posh snooty people who would laugh at a little pedlar but he said to himself, 'John, be brave.' He took his stick in his hand, put his hat on his head and set off down the long and winding roads that led to London town.

In just a few days he was standing on London Bridge. The old London Bridge with shops on it. John stared at fine ladies in silk gowns and satin petticoats. He saw gentlemen with swirling cloaks riding fine horses. But not everyone in London was rich. There were plenty of poor folk scurrying hither and thither. Between them cats and rats and even pigs wandered the streets. All day he walked up and down, down and up, but did he find anything good? Oh no. That night he slept shivering in a ditch.

The next day again John walked up and down London Bridge. He smelt the sweet perfumes of the ladies and then he smelt the nasty stench of poverty, but still he heard nothing that was any good for him. He almost went home but he stayed one more day listening to the street sellers' cries and the horses' hooves clattering on the cobblestones.

'Well, John,' he said to himself, 'now you've been brave enough to see London Bridge before you die, but you will die soon with nothing in your belly. Go home.'

Just then, a window opened above him on the bridge. A big fat red-faced man poked his head out and said, 'Oy you! Are you sellin' somfin?'

'Me?' said John. 'No, I've got nothing to sell.'

'Are you buyin' somefin?'

'Not me,' said John. 'I've not a penny to spend.'

'Are you stealin' somefin? You pickin' pockets? I seen you walkin' up and down.'

'No,' said John, 'I swear to you I'm no thief!'

'Come up 'ere!'

So John walked up the narrow stairs into the man's room. 'Eat and drink,' said the big red-faced man, 'and tell me what you're doin', 'cos I'm a curious man and I wanna know!'

On the table was a doorstep (a large hunk of bread) and on it a thick slab of cheese and beside it a great jug of beer.

John didn't need to be told twice. Hungrily he chomped on the bread and gulped down the beer and then he said, 'Maybe it sounds stupid but I'm here because of a dream. I keep having this same dream. The door opens and a man comes in wearing shining white clothes and says, "John, wake up! Go to London town and stand on London Bridge and you'll hear something good."'

Now the big, fat red-faced man began to laugh. He laughed so hard John thought he might burst and the tears were pouring down his cheeks.

'Cor blimey, John, you're the biggest twit I ever met. Ooooh! What a nutter! I mean I'm a dreamin' man meself. Only last night I 'as this dream and a boomin' voice says to me, "GO OFF TO SOME LITTLE PLACE CALLED SWAFFHAM. YOU WILL FIND A TEENY 'OUSE WIV AN APPLE TREE IN VE GARDEN. DIG UNDER IT TO FIND GOLD!" Now do you fink I'm gonna be so stupid as to go wanderin' round the countryside 'cos of a stupid dream? You listen to me, John.'

But it was too late. John was gone. He had his stick in his hand, his hat on his head and he was walking down the long and winding roads that led ... home. Then he took his spade and began digging in the dark earth under the apple tree. He dug and he dug until his spade hit something hard. And there buried in the earth was a large rusty chest. He dragged it out and prised it open. It was brim-filled with golden doubloons shining in the sun.

Now, like I said, John had a small house but a big heart. So with that money he bought himself a farm, but he also built a hospital for the poor, a park for children to play in and a church with angels carved in the roof. Many years later when he died the locals were so grateful to him that they made a statue of him, which still stands in the market place.

Under the statue it says, 'Sometimes dreams turn to gold.'

Myths from the Land of You

One day you had a dream. The dream said you should travel far, far away. You did what the dream said and there you heard about a hidden treasure. But the treasure was back at your very own home, maybe under your bed, or hidden in the walls or under the floorboards. You hurried home ...

Li Chi and Laixi

This story is from China. Some Chinese storytellers use a fan when they are telling and they make the fan transform into many different things in the tale. They know stories that take hours and hours and hours to tell, but this legend is short and sweet.

In the Yung mountains there once lived a giant snake. This serpent was twenty-five meters long and as wide as the emperor himself. Even the mightiest warriors trembled at the thought of its coiling massive body and razor-sharp teeth. To prevent it from feasting on whole villages the local officials made a deal with the monster snake. Every year a young girl of around twelve years old was delivered at the mouth of the monster's cave and never seen again.

Nine years had passed and nine girls had been taken. As the tenth year approached, the officials were looking around for a suitable girl to be the next victim. In the nearby country lived a family with six daughters. As the day approached, the youngest girl, Li Chi, woke her parents early one morning: 'Mum, Dad, please give me to the snake! It's the best thing to do. You are so poor and in return the officials will give you silver for your old age. I'm not at all scared. And after all, you do have five other daughters.' Her parents loved her dearly and refused to agree.

That night Li Chi stole secretly into her father's workshop, found his old rusty sword and sharpened it until it was keen as a razor. As she crept from the house her faithful dog Laixi followed after her. Early next morning they reached the temple, which stood near the monster's cave. Li Chi went into the temple, prayed for strength and took eight large sticky balls of rice sweetened with malt sugar. On her way out she gave one of the rice balls to little Laixi, who gobbled it up wagging his tail.

Silently they climbed to the mouth of the cave and she placed the seven remaining rice balls outside. Inside, in the darkness, the monster sniffed the luscious fragrance of sweet rice. Soon its horrible head appeared at the mouth of the cave. Its eyes gleamed like mighty mirrors, its great jaws opening wider and wider to devour the rice. At once the little dog Laixi bounded into its open mouth and took a sharp bite of its tongue. Meanwhile Li Chi ran behind with her sword and began to slice and hack deeply into the flesh of the serpent. The wounds hurt terribly; the monster leaped into the open and died in a tangled heap of coils.

Li Chi stepped up to the monstrous head and with all her strength lifted it open. Out jumped little Laixi, yapping and wagging his tail. She left him happily chewing on serpent meat and went alone into the cave. There in the darkness she found nine skulls of the girls who had come before her. She sighed as she brought them out. 'Dear sisters, because of your own terror you were devoured. I'm so sorry!'

Today brave Li Chi is still celebrated in ballads and stories, but I wonder if they remember her little dog Laixi? He had a story heart too!

If you like a tale and fancy remembering it there are games, practices and tricks that can help. You can find the bones of the story ...

Story Skeleton

- Find seven people, animals or things you think are the most important in the story.
- Write down seven action verbs; what the people or animals in the story are doing.
- Write seven feelings; the feelings of the people in the story or the feelings you have about the story.

A bit like this ...

7 nouns (things or characters)	7 verbs (actions)	7 feelings
Giant snake	Devouring	Greed
Mum and Dad	Offering	Terror
Li Chi	Planning	Love of family
Laixi	Walking	Courage
Rice balls	Finding	Creativity
Sword	Fighting	Joy
Skulls	Thinking	Sadness

As a *Natural Storyteller* you may at times wish to apply some Story Medicine. For example maybe you have a girl friend who is very nervous. This story about Li Chi might be just the thing to give her courage. I'm not saying your friend would start killing dragons, but this legend might help her realise that girls can be incredibly brave.

Johnny Appleseed

Sometimes if you look up at the clouds they seem like apple blossoms. Here's why.

There once lived a boy in America named Johnny. Johnny loved digging and playing in the mud, getting dirty and eating apples. As a lad he worked as a gardener and planted apple seeds. He had no mum, so he also looked after his little brother Nat.

One day when he was eighteen years old Johnny was leaning on his fence and heard the creaking and groaning of wagons. Soon he saw a line of prairie wagons and trotting horses.

'Where are you folks headed?' he asked.

'West. To where the forests are full to burstin' with runnin' deer, the rivers explodin' with fishes and good land ready for the takin'.'

'They have apple trees out there?' asked Johnny.

'Nope. We don't believe they do.'

'In that case I be staying right here,' said Johnny and went back to pruning the apple orchard.

However the very next day Johnny was dishing up a steaming apple pie for young Nat when he said, 'Bro, what do you think we travel on west?'

'Why in the world?' asked Nat.

'Well, bro, an angel came in my dream last night and said I was needed.'

'You needed to go west? But why, Johnny? The only thing you know anythin' about is apples.'

'That's exactly why. The angel gave me a special task of goin' west and sow-in' apple seeds everywhere I go.'

'Well in that case, I'm goin' too, Pa can look after hisself!' said young Nat.

So they went. They had no horse to ride on, no wagon to ride in and no gun to shoot with. They just filled their pockets with apple seeds and walked on their own two feet, far far away. After some time their pa moved west, built a cabin and Nat went to live with him.

But Johnny went right on walking and wherever he walked he planted apple trees.

If he came to a wooden cabin with a light in the window he knocked on the door. Though he was both dirty and dusty, he was welcomed in for his two special gifts. The first gift was that round the fire he told thrilling stories. Then next day he would be out sharing his apple seeds with the children.

'Now here's a job for you,' he'd say to them. 'You water these seeds. Once the little tree starts growin', make sure you stops the animals from munchin' them up. If they grow, why then you can go into your mom's kitchen with shiny red apples and she will surely bake you a nice apple pie.'

'Thank you, Johnny Appleseed. We sure will do what you say.' And that's how the children gave Johnny Appleseed his name.

The children usually did what they had promised. Everywhere Johnny had been, apple seeds germinated and in the spring came pinky white blossom and people would say:

'You sure can see where Johnny Appleseed's been a-walkin'. Now there's a fine fella for you.'

The years passed and the trees grew big and strong. They bore many apples and when Johnny came to visit he was welcomed as a guest of honour. 'Without you, Johnny, life would be dull and miserable. No apple pie and no apple cider.'

In those days there were almost no vegetarians but Johnny lived on food he found in nature and never ate dead animals. He never wore shoes on his feet either. Even in winter, he could walk barefoot on the snow and ice. In fact they say that the skin on his feet was so thick that a rattlesnake couldn't bite through it!

If people wanted trees from him, he refused to take money. Instead he took whatever they had, which might be bread or some old clothes, so he ended up wearing some pretty strange costumes.

Johnny learnt many First Nation languages and made friends with many tribes. So even when there was fighting between cowboys and Indians the tribes left Johnny alone. They said Johnny came from the Great Spirit.

When night fell, Johnny liked to sleep out under the stars with his cloak wrapped around him. One chilly evening he sat warming his hands on a crackling fire from twigs he'd found. Suddenly a flock of moths came fluttering right into the flames and burning their wings. Johnny jumped up, took handfuls of sand and smothered the fire. That was typical Johnny; he would rather freeze than hurt those little flying creatures.

When Johnny was getting very old, he went to stay with his brother Nat. One day, resting on the porch, he heard a rustling in the trees, and suddenly there was the angel he had dreamt about so long ago who told him to go west.

'You're to come with me, Johnny Appleseed,' said the angel. 'The Lord is waiting for you.'

'I ain't ready to go yet. I still have a whole pocketful of seeds to plant,' said Johnny.

'There's one thing you forgot,' smiled the angel. 'The Lord's garden is one of the best places you can find to plant apple seeds.'

So old Johnny took the angel's hand and left the worries of the world behind him. And they say that's why sometimes the clouds look like they are made of apple blossom: they're blooming in heaven.

Imagine you are Johnny Appleseed travelling out over the Wild West with your pockets full of apple seeds. As you digest the story, a bit of Johnny or an apple tree might start to grow in your Story Heart.

Here is the Johnny Appleseed Quiz, to help you remember his tale:
1. Who did Johnny make apple pie for?
2. Which direction were the wagons heading?
3. Who told Johnny to plant apple trees?
4. How did he carry his seeds?
5. What did the First Nation people think about Johnny?
6. What happened by the fire?
7. Why did people like Johnny Appleseed?

Myths from the Land of You

Do you know someone who is generous and kind, who puts others' comfort before their own, like Johnny? What is their story? How did it all began, once upon a time ...

Create a Story Map from Nature

- Choose a story from this book which you like.
- Go outside and collect some things. They might be stones, feathers, berries, bones of a dead mouse, seeds, drops of rainwater, anything.
- Prepare a place where you are going to make the story map. It might be a big flat stone, a piece of earth, a large log or anywhere with enough space to make your map.
- You are going to use the things you have collected to make a map that shows the whole story.

There is no right way to make the map except your way. It is up to you to do it how you want as long as it shows everything in the story. You might show it to other people but it's mainly for you to remember the story.

- As you make the map you are allowed to adapt or change the story as you wish.
- When you think it is finished, read or remember the whole story one more time to check that all the important things in the story have been included.

Now, if you want to, you can sit next to your map and tell the story to someone. You might take a photo but you don't need to. It is for you, and it will help you to remember the story so it belongs to you.

Did you solve the riddle of *Story Heart*?

You talk to me, but I have no words,
You sing to me, but I play no music,
You love me, though I am a stranger.
Who am I?

Why would you talk and sing to someone who has no words. Why would you love them even though you have only just met them? The answer is that little stranger who often says, '*Waaaaaaa!*' – a newborn baby.

Story Mind

Stories live in a galaxy called 'Mind'. You have a *Story Mind* hidden in your skull. Story Minds connect things together. Absolutely everything in the universe can connect together in a story. Rats connect to bikinis, empty tummies connect to violins (in this next story) and everything is a riddle that can be unravelled.

Here is a riddle for your *Story Mind*:

What is it that's greater than God?

What's worse than the Devil?

The dead eat it, every single day ...

But if we eat it, we die.

If you haven't found the answer by the end of *Story Mind*, it lies there. Meanwhile, the first story ...

Brian, Who Was Useless at Storytelling

Before my time, before your time and before your grandmothers' grandfathers' time there was a man called Brian and he was poor. He was as poor as a purse with no money, a heart with no love, or a storyteller with no pictures in their mind.

Brian had a job, he wove baskets. Big baskets for potatoes, medium baskets for shopping and little baskets for little girls, but on the morning I'm telling you of, Brian wasn't weaving any baskets at all because Brian had nothing to weave his baskets with. He had looked. He had looked in the hedges, in the forests, in the fields, but he couldn't find the rods he needed anywhere. There was only one place where he thought there might be some rods and that was in the Forbidden Valley.

Well, Brian had many mouths to feed: old Mother Brian and Father Brian, Mrs Brian and all the little Brians. So he put the last crust of bread in his right pocket, his knife in his left pocket and he set off. When he had reached the mouth of the Forbidden Valley he stopped. How many times had he sat beside the fire and heard his mother, his uncle and his two great-aunts saying, 'The Forbidden Valley belongs to the little people, the good people, the fairy folk. Whatever you do, never go nosying around in there!'

But what could he do? Brian had a hungry family, so he put one foot in front of the other and he walked into the Forbidden Valley. And there, sprouting in great swathes, sure enough were thousands of rods, just ready to be cut. It didn't take long before he had cut a big stack. Then he chewed on his crust and felt so drowsy that he shut his eyes. When he woke up a mist had settled over the valley, so thick that you couldn't see your hand in front of your face.

Brian was lost, more lost than he had ever been, and was thinking, why hadn't he listened to the advice? Then he saw a faint light burning in the distance, so he walked towards it. He came upon a little cottage and from the door an old woman was calling, 'Come in, Brian. Would you care for a bowl of soup?' Truth was he did care for it – very much – and soon there was no drop of soup left in his bowl.

'And now, Brian,' she said, 'do you have a story for me?'

'Oh no,' he said, 'I'm sorry I'm no good at that kind of thing. I don't know any stories at all.'

'What?' she said. 'Brian, you mean to say that even though you're in a story yourself you can't even tell one?'

'No, sorry,' he apologised.

'Well, in that case, the least you can do is pull up a bucket of water from the well.'

So Brian went out, dropped the bucket down the well and pulled it up again brimming with water. As he put it down on the flagstone he heard a rustling and a roaring, and out of nowhere a great swirling wind came and lifted him high up in the air. Amazed, Brian flew up over hedges, hills and forests.

At last the wind set him down again, beside a very long house and as the door was open he went in. Inside the house men and women dressed in black were sitting on benches along the walls. In the middle was a dead man lying in a coffin. A hearty fire was crackling in the grate and a girl with black curly hair said, 'Come in, Brian!' and poured him a big flagon of beer.

Then a tall thin man stood up, saying loudly, 'It's all very well us drinking beer but Paddy won't rest in his grave without a proper dance at his funeral. Boy, go down to the village and call the fiddler.'

At once the girl with curly black hair jumped up and said, 'Why should we go down to the village and fetch the fiddler when we have Brian, the best fiddler in Ireland, sitting right here beside me?'

Brian gasped, 'What? Me? No, I'm sorry you must have the wrong Brian. I don't know a note of music to save me life.'

Before he knew what had happened she had put the fiddle into his left hand

and the bow into his right and he was playing so merry a jig that toes were tapping and knees were bending and skirts were swirling and brows were sweating and they all said, 'Well, she was right about one thing. I've never had such a great dance in all me born days.'

Then the tall thin man stood up and said gravely, 'It's all very well us having fun, but Paddy won't rest in his grave if we don't have a proper mass at his funeral. Boy! Go down to the village and bring the priest.' But again the girl with curly black hair jumped up and said, 'Why in the world should we go down to the village and fetch the priest when we have Brian? The very best priest in the whole of Ireland is sitting right here beside me!'

Brian couldn't believe his ears. 'What, me? I know I turned out to be a bit more musical that I thought, but a priest? To be honest I can hardly even spell me own name.' But before Brian knew it he had a black cassock on his back and a prayer book in his hand and he was singing the mass and saying such beautiful prayers that tears sprang out of every eye and they sobbed and said, 'Well, she was right about one thing. I've never heard such a beautiful mass in all me born days.'

The tall, thin man stood up and said, 'It's all very well us sitting here and crying but Paddy won't rest in his grave if we don't put him there. You four boys shut the coffin and carry him down to the graveyard.' Well they shut the coffin, but when they lifted it up on their shoulders three of the men were short and the fourth was so tall that they nearly tipped poor Paddy out of his coffin. 'No, no, that won't do!' said the tall thin man. 'Boy! Go down to the village and call the doctor. We'll have to cut a bit off that man's legs. He's far too tall.'

Then the girl with the curly black hair stood up and said, 'Why should we go down to the village and fetch the doctor when we have Brian, the finest doctor the length and breadth of Ireland, sitting right here beside me?'

Well, if Brian had been pale before he was white as a sheet now and trembling from head to foot, and he said, 'What, me? No, I'm sorry, this is wrong! I admit I surprised myself there with the reading, but I can't stand the sight of blood!'

But before he knew what had happened she had put a saw in his right hand and the man's leg in his left and he was sawing away. He cut the man's leg under the knee and then he sawed over the ankle and he took a needle and thread and sewed the leg up again until it was good as new and the man stood up nice and short and they carried the coffin down the hill beautifully. Brian was just about to step over the graveyard wall when he heard a rustling and he heard a roaring and he was swept off his feet by a great wind. High up in the air he flew, above the hills and forests, streams and fields. Then the wind set him down beside the well and he took up the bucket and went inside.

'Do you have a story for me now?' asked the old woman.

'Do I have a story for you now!' said Brian. From that day Brian could do things he had never dreamt of. He went home to old Mother and Father Brian, Mrs Brian and all the little Brians and discovered that his whole family had hundreds of talents he had never noticed. And they all lived happily ever after, weaving both baskets and stories.

Myths from the Land of You

You might be like Brian – you think you're no storyteller. Maybe you just like telling stories to yourself in your own private cinema in your mind. Shut your eyes for a moment and see what kind of pictures appear. Maybe those pictures will start moving …

You can travel with your magical mind into a story. Imagine you are Brian, who has no food for his family. Imagine you are the old lady sitting in her cottage. Imagine you are Brian's kids when he gets home. See it like a film in your mind, then it will start to live and be your story.

Story Skeleton

If you want, you can make your own story skeleton for Brian's story. Think of seven things or characters in the story, then seven actions, then seven feelings. This is mine ...

7 nouns (things or characters)	7 verbs (actions)	7 feelings
Brian	Walking	Hunger
Baskets	Sleeping	Courage
Forbidden Valley	Flying	Embarrassment
Violin	Dancing	Terror
Prayer book	Crying	Astonishment
Saw	Burying	Pride
Family	Storytelling	Enjoyment

A good story is like a juicy chocolate cake. A good and delicious cake with loads of energy in it. When you eat it your tummy digests the cake. A good story is like that delicious cake. When you hear it you can either forget it, and that's that. Or you can digest it with your *Story Mind*.

The Perfect Pot

In India in olden times there were no water taps at all. Even the poshest palace in town with its golden domes had no taps. Instead there was a skinny beanstalk of a man who carried water to the palace. He put a stout stick on his shoulders with a clay pot dangling from each end. He slooshed water from the river into the pots and carried them up the path to the palace. One of his pots was perfectly rounded and always delivered a full portion of water after the long walk from the river. The other had a crack and lots of water dribbled and leaked out by the time he reached the palace.

The perfect pot was very proud and moaned about the cracked pot. 'You are a disgrace!' it said. 'Our poor water carrier has to work so hard because so much water drips out of you. You should be ashamed, you old crack-pot. At least I do my job properly.'

Finally, after years of arriving half-empty and feeling guilty, the cracked pot could stand it no longer. It said, 'Dear water carrier! I'm so sorry that I can't do what the perfect pot does.'

The water carrier stopped in his tracks. 'What do you mean?'

'You know,' said the cracked pot. 'I only deliver half my load of water. I make so much work for you because I'm no good.'

The water carrier smiled and said, 'As we walk up to the palace look at the lovely flowers along the path.'

So the pot looked and saw gorgeous flowers growing beside the path they had walked so often. The flowers stood tall and shining in the sunshine and the pot felt happier, but as they came up to the palace and the water was emptied out it said, 'Thanks for trying to cheer me up with the flowers but I'm still very sorry that I make you all that work by not being perfect.'

The water carrier shook his head. 'Dear old pot, use your imagination! Don't you understand what I'm trying to show you? Didn't you notice that the flowers only grow on one side of the path? I dropped flower seeds on your side of the path and every day you sprinkle them with water. Just the perfect amount so they can grow lush and beautiful. I could always have bought a new pot but you are perfect for this job. The flowers give joy to many a heart and home.'

The cracked pot felt so happy its crack widened into a smile. Not just new things are perfect. Old worn-out things can be perfect with a *Story Mind*.

Myths from the Land of You

There is probably a thing in your life that seems old but is very important to you. Like your dad, no, only joking. Seriously, try and think of something that is old and battered that you like and then make up a story about it. Maybe it's an old blanket that gets told off by a an ancient teddy and then starts scaring the teddy with a ghost story.

Here is a story map for 'The Perfect Pot'. Can you see the whole story? When you like a story, drawing a story map can be very enjoyable and make you understand it more. If you make a story map for 'The Perfect Pot' it will certainly be different to mine. And if you made it today it will be different from one you made yesterday. The idea is not to have it displayed in the National Gallery but to enjoy playing around with this story in your mind and on paper. You can draw it exactly as you want. You can paint it or do a collage or make an abstract drawing where you only show the colours and movements in the story. It is a good way to digest it before you tell it.

Robin Hood

When Robin Hood was young he was striding through Sherwood Forest. He was going to his first archery contest and he was excited. He knew he was good but was he good enough? Suddenly beside the path he noticed a mighty old oak tree and on its trunk a target painted bright red. Precisely at the centre of the target was an arrow. Robin realised there must be a brilliant archer travelling the same way.

As he continued walking he saw many targets and each one had an arrow at its heart. He could see from the feather fletched on the arrows that it was the same marksman who had shot each time. This archer got a bullseye every time! As he came closer Robin grew more and more nervous. He would never win against a genius like this. The sweat was running down his brow.

At last he came to a tree where the arrow was vibrating in the red target. There, beyond, was the great archer drawing his bow. He shot his arrow into a tree where there was no target.

Then he took up a paint pot and a large brush. He painted a big red target around the arrow.

The archer turned his head to young Robin, who was staring at him wide-eyed.

'Young laddie, it's not just hitting the bullseye that matters. You must learn to make your own target too!'

Every story you tell has a target. The target might be that you love the story and want to give it to someone as an invisible present. The target might be to show your friend that being the coolest archer (or football player or computer genius) is not the only important thing in the world. There are different targets. Then you can tell them the story of Robin Hood. Or the story of the Rubbish Girl ...

The Rubbish Girl

In a valley between the steep mountains of Norway there lived a prince. The king and queen fussed over their little diddums every day. The handsome boy got piles of new toys and ice cream for breakfast. So he grew up as a spoilt brat who was never satisfied with anything.

'The sun is too hot! The wind is too cold! My new cape is half a centimetre too short and my pantaloons are half a centimetre too long, you idiot!' said the prince, no matter how carefully the royal tailor had worked.

'Luckily it's ages before he will rule the kingdom,' thought the courtiers. 'Maybe he'll get nicer as he grows up.'

But the day after the prince turned eighteen the king collapsed out jogging and died of a heart attack. So the poor queen was left with an almost grown-up son who did nothing at all except argue and moan.

The queen was desperate. She told all the journalists in the kingdom that any girl who could put a stop to the prince moaning and groaning would get half the kingdom and the whole prince thrown into the bargain.

Already the same evening the palace courtyard was full of girls and women who wanted to try. They were ringing endlessly at the gilded gate, the queen didn't get a moment's peace and the prince was even more grumpy than usual. So the queen sent out a proclamation that girls who tried without success would be tattooed with the words 'I failed miserably' and it wasn't long before the whole city smelt of roasted skin.

Far off in the countryside lived a poor widow. Her three daughters thought the prince looked very cute on the pictures and how hard could it be to stop him moaning and complaining? The two eldest girls put on their best dresses, glued on false eyelashes and argued about who should use the last bit of nail varnish. Soon they were ready to totter away on their high heels.

'Wait for me,' said the youngest girl.

'There's no way you're going to traipse along after us making us look stupid,' said the older girls. 'Stay here with Mum.' But the younger sister grabbed her old school satchel, gave her mum a hug and walked barefoot after the other two.

The two older girls marched off as fast as they could in their high heels. The younger one took her time, sniffing the delicious fresh air and the smell of spring. Suddenly she called out, 'Girls, look what I've found!'

The others stopped and looked back.

'Yuk, a disgusting dead bird! You can't be serious. Put it down.'

'It's a magpie. It's beautiful; look at the rainbow shine on its feathers,' she said and she put the dead bird carefully into her schoolbag.

The older girls hurried on chattering nonstop about everything brilliant they would say to the prince. Then they heard, 'Look!'

The two older girls sighed. 'What is it now?'

'A stick!'

'Fantastic, you found a stick in the forest! Let's call the bank manager. That must be worth a million pounds.'

'But this is a specially nice stick,' replied their sister, grinning, and she put it in the schoolbag with the magpie.

They hadn't walked much further when they heard, 'Hey, look what I found! This is fantastic. An old plate!'

'Stop picking up rubbish. Drop it. It's filthy and worthless,' said the older girls.

But the youngest sister cleaned the plate lovingly with a bit of bright green moss and put it into her bag.

The sun was climbing higher in the sky and the two older girls stomped onwards in silence, wondering how much further it could be. The youngest sister ambled along looking right and left at everything that was growing in the forest and suddenly she cried out, 'Looook!'

'What is THAT?'

The younger sister held it up. 'A truly huge pair of underpants!'

'Put them down at once!'

'But they are so massive. I wonder who lost them? They must have had an enormous bum,' she said, carefully folding them into her bag.

Before long she was shouting loudly, 'It's my lucky day today!'

The two older girls looked at each other and said, 'Give us a break!'

'Wait, have a look! You are going to be amazed by this!'

She held up a curly ram's horn.

'Yuk! It's probably full of diseases, rotten inside and stinking.'

'It smells fine. I'm going to keep it. But wait, hold on a minute. You'll never believe it—'

The two older sisters shouted together, 'WHAT IS IT NOW?'

'Another one! It must be from the same sheep. Isn't it beautiful?' she said.

'NO!' shouted the sisters. 'It's old-fashioned, disgusting and stinky. Throw it away this very minute!'

'Sorry if you're jealous. I can share if you want,' she said and popped them both into her bag.

They carried on in silence. The two older girls had got blisters from their high-heeled shoes and were in a bad mood. At last the palace came in sight.

They walked over the grass with the younger sister trailing along behind.

'Oho! Well I never did!' she said.

Furious, the two older sisters stopped and glared back at her.

'That's it! We happen to be going into the royal palace right now. Everyone will call you "Rubbish Girl" and someone might think we are in the same family. From now on you are not to say a single word to us. We are going to act like we never ever saw you before. Get it?'

'OK. I just want to say one last thing. Look at this jogging shoe! I wonder who left it here? Maybe it was the one the king used on his very last jog. In that case he had pretty worn-out old trainers. Look there's a hole in it.'

There was no answer. She took the shoe and put it into her old school satchel.

At the palace was a line of young ladies. At the front was a princess. A servant was fluffing up her hair with silver hairspray. Behind her a giant lady was standing and practising a speech in a booming loud voice. Then came a girl reading feverishly through a thick pile of books. Beside her was a girl in a red kung fu suit who shouted 'HAI!' so loudly that all the others jumped. The last one had a golden dress and a whole choir who sang, 'Bettina is the best!' as she pushed towards the front of the queue.

The three sisters waited at the back of the queue. One after the other the girls went in. One after the next they came out again, weeping from the tattoo.

At last it was the turn of the oldest sister to be shown through the huge front door.

Inside the palace it was hot. The prince lay on the sofa, eating ice cream.

'Oy, it's warm in here,' she said.

'It's hotter in the fire,' said the prince.

She turned and saw the crackling hot fireplace. Then she saw the tattoo needles, still steaming from the last girl, and all the clever and funny things she had planned to say flew out of her head like a flock of birds. So you can imagine it didn't take long before she was tattooed too.

Then it was the turn of the middle sister. In she came and there was the handsome prince lying there and eating ice cream.

'Goodness, it's boiling in here.'

'It's hotter in the fire,' said the prince in an irritated tone.

She turned and saw the fire crackling fiendishly and the tattoo needles glowing in the coals. She too forgot all her clever ideas and in no time was hurrying out with a mark on her skin.

Now it was the turn of the youngest sister.

'Nice and warm in here,' she said.

'Not another idiotic girl – they all say the same thing. It's hotter in the fire!' said the prince.

'Perfect for roasting my dead bird then,' said the girl and she took the magpie out of her bag. She began to pluck it so the feathers flew around the room and the prince just stared at her, hardly believing his eyes.

'Um, you can't possibly roast a disgusting dead bird in here. You'll burn your fingers.'

'That was kind of you,' she said, 'but luckily I've brought this beautiful stick with me.' She pulled out her stick, stuck it through the bird and started to barbeque it on the posh fireplace.

The prince glared at her for a moment, then said, 'You're not going to be allowed to borrow any of my golden plates, you know, to eat it off.'

'I wouldn't dream of being so cheeky, Your Majesty,' she said, smiling. 'But luckily I found this plate on the path. Look it's got a nice blue picture on even though it's a bit chipped on the edge.' And she took the plate out of her bag to show him.

The smell of the roasting bird was getting quite delicious and the prince was getting hungry after eating ice cream all day.

'You will be thrown out at once if you let any fat or dirt spill onto my priceless silk carpet,' he said.

'Not to worry. I'll just mop it up with this,' she said and she waved in the prince's face the massive pair of underpants she'd found.

The prince stared in disbelief. For a few moments he was silent, his mouth hanging open. Then he said, 'Where on earth did you get them? They must be a troll's underpants. Look, you girl, you're just twisting every word I say with those weird things in your satchel!'

'Oh no, don't worry, your words are not twisted. If you want to see something that's really twisted, take a look at this!' And with that she pulled out the big curly ram's horn to show him.

'I ... I, I've never seen anything like it!' he stuttered.

'Haven't you? Well here it is. Look, exactly the same,' she said as she took out the other one.

'You're ... you're ... you're wearing me out,' said the prince, jumping up and dropping his ice cream on the silk carpet.

'You don't look worn out; you look rather handsome, if you don't mind me saying. But, if you want to see something that's really worn out, look at this!' And she brought the worn-out old trainer up from her bag.

The prince went quiet.

'Now, you're mine!' said the youngest sister. So she got a crown on her head and half the kingdom into the bargain. And she took the prince out, taught him to climb trees and showed him all the fun you can find in the forest. So they lived ... happily ever after of course!

Snip snap sun,
That story is done!

Myths from the Land of You

Pick up some random objects at home or at a friend's. How can this broken football or wonky umbrella be useful? Imagine that those things are just what is needed – the football can be used as a little cushion for a tired devil on his way home and then the wonky umbrella comes in handy when the big bully devil tries to beat him up. Choose your things and then weave a story.

True or False?

1. The prince loved ice cream.
2. The queen was very strict with her son and he always had to do seventeen press-ups before breakfast.
3. If the girls failed to shut up the prince they would get a tattoo.
4. The two oldest sisters adored their little sister and called her their sweet darling pet.
5. The youngest sister collected stamps.
6. The youngest girl picked up seven things on the path.
7. After waiting out in the cold, the girls got put off by the warm fire.

Did the youngest sister in this story look like you or someone you know? That's up to your *Story Mind*. My dad once surprised me by saying that if he heard Cinderella or a story about a princess he always used to imagine himself as her. One thing's for sure, that girl was a talented recycler.

Minding the Way

Next to a blue waterhole in Willeroo in deepest Australia lived a tiny girl called Maree. Maree followed her gran around all day. Gran was seriously old, her skin was lined and wrinkled and her eyes were twinkly in her head. Gran knew every living and breathing thing in Willeroo.

One evening after the sun went down and it was very dark Gran went out walking. All Maree's aunties and cousins followed her walking into the darkness. Maree was excited and scared at the same time and she ran and held tight to Gran's hand. Gran had no map or GPS; instead she kept staring up at the stars and they told her the way.

When they got to Sugar Mountain everyone lay down on their backs and looked up at the starry sky. Gran knew the stories of every star in the sky, but this night she told Maree's favourite story – about the star who had once been a beautiful naughty child.

Then they stood up and sang. They sang as they walked. Maree knew some of the songs and the ones she didn't know she just hummed along to. They sang the rocks and they sang the green wattle sweeties and the lilli pilli fruits. They sang the Wongan cactus and they sang the carving that Uncle had cut into the big black kurrajong tree. Then they sang Emu's name – 'Tarrawingie! Tarrawingie! Tarrawingie! Tarrawingie! Tarrawingie!'

The emus must have heard them! All of a sudden emus came running by, huge birds with long legs. Then Maree saw that some of them were not really birds; they were men. Their bodies were painted with white clay shining in the dark. They were dancing the emu dance and Maree was half giggling and half scared as they charged around fast like big strutting emus.

Gran had found an emu egg, so they made a fire to cook it on. One emu egg is like twenty chickens' eggs and with some other goodies they had a delicious feast. Oh, Maree loved to go walking with Gran.

Now Maree is a gran herself. At night she walks around without a map and her grandchildren follow her. The stars and the stories show her the way.

In Australia, the Aboriginal people sometimes sing as they walk – maybe for hundreds of kilometres. They sing everything on the walk. In their tradition, they don't sing about something; they say the sound of their voice becomes the spirit of the thing. They sing the stones, the water-holes and things that happened there long ago in mythical time. They say song helps to keep the land alive.

You might want to find your own songline for a place near you. But before you do that, here is a songline game ...

Songline Game

You can play this with one other person or lots of other people. Everyone who is playing should find a treasure. A stone, money, sweets or any kind of treasure. You secretly hide your treasure somewhere fairly close by. Then you make up a rap, a poem or a songline to explain how to find it.

For example:

- Jump up off your bum
- You lazy thing.
- Clean out your ears
- And hear me sing!
- Walk down the steps
- With a one two three.
- Turn to the left
- And what do you see?
- Climb up high,
- As high as you can.
- Then you'll find a treasure
- That's my secret plan.

Your songline might be a lot better or longer than this one. Sing or rap it to the others and enjoy watching them try to follow your song and get to the treasure.

Make Your Own Songline

You can do this alone or with friends.

1. First choose a place near you that you would like to make a songline for.
2. Then simply sit down quietly and think about that place. It's like you are telling it you are going to visit.
3. If it's warm enough, take off your shoes.
4. Walk slowly to the place, stopping as often as you wish, looking around and listening.
5. Maybe you will hear part of the songline. You may hear someone else singing it, a bird may be singing it, the leaves may be whispering it or perhaps you will sing it yourself.
6. At first you may be a bit embarrassed or unsure about singing to a place. Relax, feel the wind on your skin, the ground under your feet. You can just start by humming. You don't need to sing words. But when you hum it may help you to be in the land in a different way. This is not about making a brilliant song. Take your time, stop if you want, sing quiet, chant, do a loud yodel, whatever you feel like.
7. Maybe you will sing, maybe not, maybe you won't even hear a bird or a tree whisper the song today. Still you might find you know the place better and remember it for the rest of your life.

Now you have entered the country of *Story Mind*. The mind of a storyteller. Did you guess the answer to the riddle?

> *What is it that's Greater than God?*
>
> *What's worse than the Devil himself?*
>
> *The Dead eat it, every single day ...*
>
> *And if we eat it, we die?*

There is only one thing that's greater than God and worse than Old Nick: the favourite food of dead things. The answer – Nothing.

Story Tree

In spring I dress bright

As I reach to the light.

In summer more clothing I wear.

When colder it grows,

I fling off my clothes,

And in winter quite naked appear.

What am I?

Did you guess the answer to that riddle? If so, your *Story Mind* is developing fast! You will become a *Natural Storyteller* before you know it. In order for this to happen, the next step in your training is – become a tree. This is a hard step, a stumbling block for many a pompous human being who thinks they are the most important thing in the world. Have they forgotten that without trees they can't breathe a single breath?

So study *Story Tree*. If you read too many stories at once, you might get constipation and lose your appetite. So between each tale put the book down. Visit a real tree – they are the experts.

The Bundle of Sticks

One day three sisters were fighting, pulling each other's hair and screaming. Their mother was so fed up she called out, 'Girls! Go out this minute and bring me a bundle of sticks tied together with string.'

The girls dashed outside. 'Hey, elephant nose! Give that stick to me!'

'No way, cushion bum! I got it first.'

'You two are so babyish!' said the oldest. 'Look at your sticks – all bent and silly!'

Finally they came in and gave the bundle of sticks to their mother.

'Thank you,' said the mother. 'Now, take the bundle and break it in half.' She gave it to the youngest girl.

The youngest girl couldn't break the bundle. So the mum handed it to the middle girl. She strained and tried with all her might but couldn't even bend the bundle.

'Hey you weaklings!' said the oldest grabbing the sticks. She puffed and gasped but there was no way she could break it either.

Then their mum took the bundle, untied the string and handed each girl a single stick. 'See if you can break that.' They took the sticks and snapped them in half as easy as pie.

'My darlings!' said their mum. 'The more you quarrel and are divided like these sticks, the more easily you can be broken. Stop arguing and stay together like a bundle of sticks, like sisters. Then no one can hurt you, you will be so strong.'

From that day on the three sisters stayed united, looking after one another like twigs on the same tree.

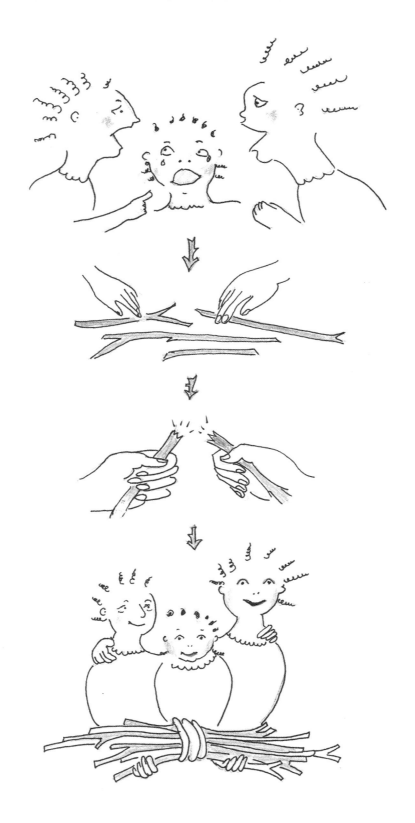

Myths from the Land of You

Re-tell this story as if the three sisters were you and your friends, brothers or sisters. Who would tell you to get the twigs? What does it feel like when someone tells you off?

If I want to practise a story and there is no one around to tell it to, sometimes I tell it to a tree. First I check that no one is looking at me or they might think I am really weird. In fact, maybe they think that anyway. Then I tell the story and one thing is for sure – trees can make very good listeners. Maybe that's because, like they say in Estonia and in many places, trees have spirits living in them.

St Peter and the Oak Tree

One day St Peter and God were out strolling over the earth to see how things were. That day the sun was shining and sparkling on the leaves and the birds were tweeting blissfully but St Peter was in a terrible mood. I don't know why he was angry; maybe he had blisters on his toes or had missed breakfast? He stomped along past flowers and trees.

Then they came to a meadow where a large oak tree stretched its branches up towards the light. St Peter marched over to the tree and threw himself into the shade.

'Would you like a drink?' asked the Lord. 'I have a bottle of milk. It's a bit sour but it's not bad.'

'No!' said St Peter, irritably and stared up at the large oak leaves.

It went quiet. St Peter lay and thought how rubbish the world was. He was hungry and thirsty and all he could see was inedible grass and stupid acorns.

At last he blurted out, 'You made so many blunders when you created the plants! Someone should tell you. Look at this oak tree, for example. Absolutely useless, ridiculous little nuts that taste disgusting. And then you made melons which are so much work to plant in the garden. This huge tree would be so much better if it grew melons – why just this one tree would have more melons than a whole farm does. How could you make such a stupid mistake?'

'I didn't make the oak tree for the sake of the acorn,' answered the Lord quietly. 'I made it for itself. But pigs think acorns are delicious – they are very nutritious – people use the bark to tan leather and the wood is used for both ships and floors. If an oak tree is left alone it can live a thousand years and be home to many wonderful insects. I would say oak is a great creation. A king of the forest.'

St Peter sighed deeply. 'Well, obviously it can be handy for this and that but why don't you listen to what I say for once? An acorn is an acorn, you must admit that. And melons are melons, something quite different. And which is the biggest is pretty obvious. If only acorns were melons they would be a suitable fruit for a tree like this. The tree must be really ashamed of those pitiful small nuts.'

'Hmm,' answered the Lord and touched the tree. The oak trembled, the crown whispered, the branches sank and suddenly the tree was full of melons. Hundreds of melons, watermelons as big as car tires and honey melons the size of footballs hung all over the tree. St Peter gasped.

'Was that what you had in mind?'

'Y-y-yes!' stammered St Peter.

'Are you satisfied now?'

'Am I satisfied? This is fantastic! This is the best tree I have ever seen. Just perfect!

'You don't think the melons are a bit on the big side?' asked the Lord.

'Not at all, not at all,' said St Peter and jumped up to pick one.

At that moment one of the largest melons came loose and began to fall. It hit St Peter and since it was perfectly ripe it cracked open over his head down to his shoulders. There it sat like a massive bucket stuck on his head over his eyes, mouth and ears. He ran around swishing his arms here and there and banging into the tree.

At last he gave a desperate tug, while kicking out like a wild horse. It looked like he was pulling off his whole head, but the melon flew off and dropped to the ground.

He spat out the melon pips and took a deep breath. 'Get those melons down, another one might fall down and kill someone!' He stood trembling and shivering and melon juice ran down his face. 'Quickly, I tell you! I was wrong. It was a very bad idea.'

'Very well,' said God quietly and lay his hand on the trunk. 'Let it be.'

There stood the oak tree quietly with its green leaves and round small acorns. Every acorn sat in its own little cup, peeped out between the twigs and glorified the tree in its simple way.

'How lovely,' thought St Peter. 'Actually the acorns really suit the tree.'

Have you ever seen a real oak tree? Even better, have you ever climbed an oak tree? Climbing trees is a bit like telling stories: good to start with smaller ones.

Myths from the Land of You

Tell yourself the story of when you felt like St Peter, really fed up and bored out of your mind. Then you climbed a tree and that changed the way you felt. Because of someone you met in the tree, because of the tree itself, or something else …

All in the Family

The story of evolution tells that the world was covered in slime for about 2.6 billion years! Slime, slime and more slime.

During those 2.6 billion years the slime turned very slowly into tiny one-celled organisms. We call them eukaryotic cells. These very little beings are too small for us to see but they are covered with a kind of skin like us, and have their own teeny backbone. They have their own way of digesting food and reproducing themselves; they are almost like tiny people. During the next billion years those eukaryotic cells began to join together to make bigger and bigger living beings. Algae, plants, fish, trees, birds and animals.

This evolution story says that our ancestors the apes lived in the tree-tops for eighty million years. That must have been fun, throwing our hairy bodies from branch to branch, with a baby ape clinging to our chest. Then some of the apes dropped down to the ground and eventually became us, the kind of animal called human beings.

According to this story we have the same ancestors as the trees – those tiny one-celled eukaryotic beings. And it makes total sense. Why else would we be so similar to trees?

You come from a seed
That your mum and dad planted together.
And a tree comes from a seed, like an apple or a nut.

You're covered in a layer of soft skin, from your head to your toes.
And a tree's skin is bark from the tips of its roots to the ends of its twigs.

You are filled with red blood,
And a tree is filled with clear sap.

You have a trunk,
A tree has a trunk.

You have arms,
A tree has branches.

On the top of your head is a crown,
A tree has a far greater crown than that.

Beside your heart are two lungs, they look like small trees.
When you breathe out, the tree breathes in,
And when the tree breathes out, you breathe in!

Charles Darwin first published the evolution story – his theory of evolu-tion – in 1859. He called it On the Origin of Species. *This story changed the world in a big way.*

All over the world there are forests – now we are going to a deep dark endless forest in Russia …

The Birch Tree

Once long ago a poor soldier was walking through the endless forests of Russia. Dark trees towered tall above him as he trod the narrow path. Then he spied a light shining far off in the distance. As he came nearer he saw the light was a little red devil sitting on a tree stump.

'Hallo, soldier!' grinned the little devil. 'Going home? No! You don't have a home, do you? You have no father or mother, no sister or brother. So why not work for me?'

'What kind of work would that be?' asked the soldier, trying not to let the devil see how sad he was.

'It's easy – just go up that hill and you will see three tents. In each tent is a falcon. Guard those birds!'

The soldier didn't like the devil's dirty little red face one bit. But he had no place to go and no job either, so he agreed. The devil laughed, stretched out its red leathery wings and flew off to fetch a money bag.

The soldier walked up to the hill where three tents flapped in the wind. He marched up to the first tent, lifted the door and inside was a cage. In the cage was a brown falcon beating its wings furiously. Its eyes shone like brass and tears of blood coursed down its feathery cheeks. Every now and then the bird threw itself violently against the bars of the cage.

'Hey, brown falcon, take it easy!' said the soldier and went to the second tent.

Therein lay a silver cage and in it a pure white falcon. The bird stood still. Then it opened its brilliant silver eyes, looked at the soldier with great sadness and closed them again.

In the third tent was a golden cage and a falcon shining like a tiny sun. As the soldier entered it turned away, refusing to look him in the eyes. 'Hey golden falcon, it's not my fault you're trapped in a cage,' he said and he went out. He was tired so he sat under a pretty silver birch tree growing on top of the hill.

As if from nowhere a voice rang out: 'Soldier, what do you work for, pleasure or money?'

The soldier looked around but could see no one. 'I work for money. Who is asking?'

'It's me, the birch tree. I'm sorry I have no money to give you.'

'Do you have a job for me?'

'Yes. It's quite simple. Just follow your heart.'

The soldier thought there was no harm in trying so he listened to his heart. It seemed to tell him he was hungry. So he got out a chunk of dry bread and a raw onion and ate. Again he listened. His heart seemed to tell him to drink, so he went down to the babbling brook and drank.

Then he listened to his heart again. He jumped up and went into the first tent. The bloodstained falcon was flapping and fussing and tearing at the bars with its talons and glancing furiously at the soldier.

'Poor handsome thing, stuck in a cage, can't even see the light of day.' Glancing out to see if the devil was near, the soldier opened the cage door. The bird stormed out and threw itself on the soldier, tearing at his cheeks until they bled.

At last he ripped the bird off his face and it flew away. The soldier burst into tears and sat on the ground, blood dripping from his wounds. Above him the falcon sat in the birch tree and glared down at him.

'Well, have you done your duty?' asked the soft voice of the tree.

'Yes and look at the thanks I got.'

At this the soldier looked up at a fork in the tree. Pushing out of the bark appeared the head of a girl.

'Take this!' she called and sap dripped down from the twigs onto his face and the gashes and wounds on his cheeks healed at once.

Sitting under the tree again the soldier found himself listening to his heart. Looking this way and that to see if the devil was near, he jumped up and into the second tent. The silver falcon sat as still as stone, staring solemnly ahead. He opened the cage but still the bird sat and didn't move, so he reached in and took it out. From his arms, it stretched wide its wings and flew out through the door and up onto a branch.

In the fork of the birch tree the girl gasped as she pulled herself out of the tree up to her waist.

'Come on, come right out!' called the soldier.

'I can't. I'm not strong enough.'

'Oh well, I can't stop listening now,' said the soldier and he plunged into the third tent.

In the gilded cage he saw the back of the golden falcon. Looking to right and to left nervously in case the devil was in sight, the soldier opened the cage. He tried to pull the bird out. Alas, it was fiery hot, it was burning his fingers. He tore strips from his shirt and wound them around his hands. Then he reached in and held the golden falcon even though his fingers felt red hot. As he pulled it out the falcon turned its golden gaze on him and in a moment the soldier was blinded. Outside, it flew up and away and the soldier fell to the ground.

'Soldier man, are you still alive?' came the soft voice of the birch tree girl.

'Yes I'm alive but I'm blinded. Is that what I get for following my heart?'

Lying on the earth, the soldier saw nothing but darkness. Above him he heard the flapping of wings and felt a large bird land on his chest. Something wet was dripping into his face. His eyes stung and he opened them to see a blinding light. In another moment he saw it was the silver falcon sitting on his chest, its tears washing onto his face. He could see!

He jumped to his feet and saw the girl climbing out of the birch tree. She stood before him, her shirt white as the bark of the tree, her eyes dark like the blemishes on the bark and her skin rosy pink like the inside of the bark when you peel it off. On her right shoulder sat the brown falcon, on her left shoulder the golden falcon and in her arms she held the silver.

The soldier was about to speak when the sky darkened.

'Run!' he called. 'It must be the devil. He won't be happy when he sees the birds are free.'

Sure enough, through the clouds came the red devil flying rapidly closer and soon they heard the sound of leathery wings flapping furiously.

The soldier took up his gun and aimed but it was impossible to see into the dark thundery sky. What to do? Shutting his eyes but following his heart he shot into the mass of gathering clouds.

At this the clouds burst and the rain fell and then just as suddenly it cleared and the devil was nowhere to be seen. The soldier turned and looked at the girl standing before him, soaking wet, and beside her three young men, one with brown hair, one with flaming golden hair and the third with silver white. They were all dripping wet from the rain but they were all laughing.

'These are my brothers. Our enchantment is broken. We live nearby,' said the birch tree girl. They took the soldier by the hand and led him into the deep dark endless forest. And there they lived together in great happiness and contentment.

Is everything in the story included in this map? If you want to remember, read the story and then make a story map for yourself.

Do you know a birch tree? Maybe you already do; it's one of the easiest to recognise with its black and white bark. Every single birch tree is different from every other one. Maybe you can find one that reminds you of the tree in the story. In the spring you can make tea from its leaves and it will clean your body, and you can also collect the sap, which tastes delicately sweet. It could be nice to tell the story beside a birch tree, but make sure you know it well and have tried it out a few times before you do. Telling stories outside can be harder than inside, but if you suceed it is more powerful.

Hodja

There's a man called Hodja. Some say Hodja comes from Turkey; other people say he is from Iran or Afghanistan. One thing is for sure – stories about Hodja are told all over the world. Some people say he is very wise and other people say he is very silly.

They say that when Hodja was old, rather fat and not as fit as he used to be he went out, dug a great pit and planted a tree in front of his house.

'Hodja, who has tricked you into planting trees at your age?' called a group of young women who were passing by. One of them laughed and said, 'You're so stupid, Hodja, that's a pistachio tree. Don't you know that it takes thirty years to get nuts from a tree like that? You're never even going to taste one of them. You're wasting your time!'

'Hodja's old and daft,' scoffed another. 'Look at that little cherry tree he's planted over there. He probably won't even be alive when it blossoms!'

Hodja took no notice but carried on digging, planting first one tree and then another, pressing the earth firmly around each one and tying up a stake for it to lean on as it grew. At last he straightened up his back, looked straight at the young women and smiled.

'I'm not planting them for myself, ladies. I'm planting them for your children.'

As well as in Turkey, Iran and Afghanistan, Hodja stories get told in Syria, Iraq, Pakistan, Bulgaria, America, France and loads and lots of other places. If you like Hodja you can collect Hodja stories and swap them with other people who are Hodja fans.

True or False?

1. Hodja stories are told only by ghosts in the middle of the night.
2. Hodja was keen to plant trees even though he was old and fat.
3. There were a lot of old ladies in the village who were trying to steal Hodja's donkey.
4. It takes many years before a nut tree starts bearing nuts.
5. Hodja planted only nut trees.
6. Hodja was planting trees to earn lots of money selling the nuts.

Myths from the Land of You

Those young women thought Hodja was old and stupid. Really old people may have had some great adventures in their life. But they can be a bit shy to tell you, as people maybe don't ask them very often about when they were young. You need to be patient and listen well, nodding your head and saying 'yes', and asking them to explain more about whatever they tell you.

The Tun Tree

Long ago and long ago it was. In the far north of Norway lived a little family. Outside their wooden house grew a tall and mighty tree. How many years it had been there nobody knew but people could see it from far and wide.

The little family loved the tree and on feast days and holidays they always remembered to share their celebration with it, pouring beer over its roots or hanging ribbons on its branches. There they lived together in peace and contentment, a mother, a father and their child. They had a little forest farm, two cows and seven goats. Not far off lived a grand family. Tall they were, proud and rich from mining precious stones out of the mountain. They thought the little family were too miserable and poor even to speak to.

One day, the girl came in as she did each day, carrying her bucket filled to the brim with clean clear shining water from the well. Her father and mother sat by the fire. They called her over and said, 'Dearest child, today the doctor came by. He says we are very ill and will surely die. Please don't be frightened. You won't be alone. The great tree that stands by the house will look after you. Trust the tree; it will not fail you.'

Just as they said, the mother and father grew pale and thin and one day they walked out into the forest and the girl knew they would not come back. So she sat alone in her little wooden house and cried as if there were two small streams running down her cheeks.

Suddenly she remembered what her mother and father had told her. She went outside and sat with her back against the trunk of the tree. She looked up and saw hundreds and thousands of shining pine-needles dancing in the wind. And they seemed to say to her, 'Dear child, don't worry about your mother and father. They are at peace now.' Then birds flew down to the tree and sang to her the joys of the skies. And her two cows and seven goats sat around the tree too. She stopped crying and wondered at the spirit of the tree.

As she sat under the tree that afternoon she saw her rich neighbours sneaking in and nosying about in her house. They dragged out all her furniture and then some of them even moved into the house, but she thought, 'I don't need a house any longer. I have the tree.'

As evening fell the branches of the tree seemed to lean down over her, protecting her from the night.

The next morning she woke to find the neighbours standing in a circle around her saying, 'This girl, she has no father and mother, she has no furniture and no house and still she is contented. It's not normal. It's disgraceful! It must be because of this tun tree.' They ran off and fetched their sharp-toothed saws and cut down the branches of the tree and the sound of the sawing was, 'Hzz! Hzz! Hzz!'

The girl watched them sawing. It looked as if they were shaving off all the beautiful hair of her tree and she fell against the trunk of the tree, crying. But as she touched the bark she heard a voice inside the tree saying, 'I am the trunk of the tree. I have been standing here for over two hundred years. I have seen people coming and going. Some are cruel like these neighbours and some are like your mother and father, full of kindness. Never fear, child. I will take care of you.'

Again the girl dried her tears. Meanwhile the neighbours stood staring at her and said, 'Look at that girl. She has no father and mother, no furniture and no house. Her tree has no branches and still she is peaceful. It's shocking and shameful! It must be the trunk of the tun tree.' So they scurried off and fetched their axes and they hacked and chopped at the ancient tree bole and the sound of their chopping went, 'Ch! Ch! Ch!' and the great trunk fell crashing to the ground.

The girl couldn't bear to see them hurt the great tree and she threw herself down beside the tree trunk, weeping. But it so happened that she fell with her ear down on the roots of the tree, and she stopped crying and listened. From deep under the earth she heard, 'We are the roots of the tree. We know secrets that human beings haven't even dreamt of. Don't fret, my child, we will care for you.' And the girl rolled over onto her back and looked up at the bright blue sky and smiled.

Then the neighbours formed a tight circle round the girl and they said to one another in maddened voices, 'Look, look at that child! No father, no mother, no furniture, no branches, no trunk and still she's not crying! It's not normal. It must be the roots of the tree!' They scampered off and fetched their spades and dug out the roots and struck a light. Soon sharp red tongues of fire were licking at the roots and the smoke billowed into the girl's eyes and tears streamed down her face.

As she stood staring at the fire suddenly she saw an abundance of scarlet sparks soaring up into the air. The sparks turned into ashes and floated away in the wind. As they flew the ashes called out, 'Don't worry about those stupid neighbours. Come with us!'

So the girl laughed and ran after the ashes. Out of the forest came the two cows and the seven goats and they ran along with her.

Then the neighbours went crazy with anger and they dropped their tools and ran after the girl and her animals. They ran and ran and ran. They ran through a day and a night and the next morning they came to the great blue fjord, and the neighbours were so angry that they kept on racing out into the cold salt water and that was the end of them.

The girl shook her head and sat down by the water. Beside her the cows and the goats grazed peacefully. The girl watched the ashes floating down through the clear water to the seabed. There before her very eyes the ashes turned into seeds which sprouted fast. In no time at all they had grown into trees rising up from the water. On the trees swelled luscious cones, shiny and sweet smelling.

The girl reached out, picked one of the cones and cracked it open. Inside were little creamy nuts which tasted delicious. She filled her arms with cones and walked with her animals along the beach until she came to a little fishing village. She laid down the heap of cones in the centre of the village and called out, 'Come and eat!' Soon all the villagers were eating nuts and said, 'This is really tasty! What's it called?' and she said, 'Well if you don't know and I don't know let's call them pine nuts.' They laughed and asked the girl to dinner.

In that village the girl lived happily. Her animals lived there too and had many calves and kids. When she was a very old woman she would sit in the shade of the trees by the water. Children would often play around her. They loved to take the cones and play with them, making them into animals and birds. Every now and then she would reach over, take one of the pine cones, crack it open and say; 'Eat, children! Eat with respect. Remember, these trees are like a father and mother to me and you.'

Tun Tree Quiz

1. Where do the little family live and who lives with them?
2. What do the parents say to their child?
3. What does the girl do when her mum and dad don't come back?
4. What happens when the neighbours cut down the tree trunk?
5. Where does the girl run to?
6. What were inside the cones?
7. In the end of the story is the girl angry and bitter about what happened?

If you are reading this, you have finished *Story Tree*. Congratulations – it was a big task but a must for the *Natural Storyteller*. How would you like to have your own tree?

In many places people plant their own tree in their garden. This tun tree is often called the Guardian Tree and is a bit like a member of the family. On special occasions like Christmas, they feed the tree some of the festival dinner or pour milk or beer over its roots.

In ancient times in many places justice also took place under a mighty old tree. Some people have said that the beech tree is the best place for justice, as it's impossible to tell a lie under this beautiful tree. In Finland families took off a bit of bark from their tun tree and wrote on the trunk important things that happen in the family. They said that it protected the family.

Some say that the reason they like to have a tun tree in their garden or on their farm is that it reminds them of Yggdrasil. Who is Yggdrasil?

In Norway, where I live, they tell of the huge World Tree whose name is Yggdrasil. At the top of this tree sits an eagle and on the top of the eagle's head sits a falcon. Those birds keep a sharp eye on everything in the nine worlds. At the bottom of the tree are three roots. One root goes down into the world of the gods, the second root goes to the world of the giants and the third into our world. A squirrel called Ratatosk runs up and down the tree passing messages from top to bottom and back. When Odin, the father of the gods wanted wisdom, he hung himself upside down from the World Tree Yggdrasil and after nine days he fell down and picked up the runes, the Viking alphabet.

How to Plant or Adopt Your Own Tun Tree

There are many ways to do this.

1. One way is to look around and find a tree that grows near where you live and adopt that tree. It's a good plan to find out who owns it and ask if you can adopt it. Then you will need to ask the tree if it wants to be part of your family. You might want to make a party to invite the tree to be your tun tree. Perhaps, like the people of Devon do with their apple trees, you will give it a nice drink. Perhaps, like the people of Greece, you will make some decorations to hang on the tree. Or perhaps you will sing to it or climb up into the branches and have a little chat. Trees are pretty quiet but they make fantastic listeners and you might find they have some good advice for you too.

2. The second way to make a tun tree is to grow one. Do you have space for a tree in your garden or does your class know someone who has room for a tree?

What kind of tree? Investigate how big trees can grow. Any tree can become a tun tree, but perhaps there is one kind of tree you like especially. You might want to take the nut or the seed and germinate it yourself, but remember, some trees need to be in a cold place like outside or a fridge to germinate.

3. Another way is to go to a place where there are lots of 'tree children', or small saplings growing tightly together. Again, it's good practice to ask the little sapling before you dig it up. If it's an oak tree, the chances are it will be delighted to get its own space; they love to have plenty of room to stretch out their limbs.

Then you need to dig a deep pit and add some good soil so the tree will have plenty of room to stretch out its roots. It's a good idea to protect it from nibblers like rabbits and put in a good stake so you don't forget where it is. Then ... don't forget to water it. If it's still alive in a year's time you can hold a birthday party for your very own tun tree. If you are lucky and it survives, it may grow to be a thousand years old.

Did you get the answer to the *Story Tree* riddle?

In spring I dress bright
As I reach to the light.
In summer more clothing I wear.
When colder it grows,
I fling off my clothes,
And in winter quite naked appear.
What am I?

The answer is ... a tree (a deciduous tree not a needle tree).

Story Animal

Now to the animal kingdom. You may have already realised that you are also an animal. OK, you probably don't pounce off branches onto mice or live in a cage. But the fact you know that you are a human kind of animal will be extremely helpful when you tell stories of other beasts and creatures.

Here the training is getting a bit harder. In this section there are two riddles to answer:

1. I jump when I walk and I sit where I stand. What am I?

2. You are standing very near to a mammal. You walk one kilometre to the south. Then you walk one kilometre to the west. Then you walk one kilometre due north. Oh my goodness, you are back next to the same animal. Which animal is it?

You have recently turned yourself into a tree (in your mind) but trees are not that good at riddles. They are fantastic at turning carbon dioxide into oxygen and have many other talents but riddles is not one of them. So just relax, enjoy *Story Animal* and come back to the riddles if the answers don´t pop into your mind ...

The Medicine Bear

In the land of snow and Northern Lights, lived a Sami family. They loved their three sons, each one tougher than the last. Then the mother had a little girl. The parents were so happy they no longer seemed to see their boys and the two older lads began to hate the little maid. When their mother's back was turned they teased her and mocked her heartlessly.

As she grew older the two older boys taunted her so much that one morning she could bear it no more. She put on her warm gákti (traditional clothes for both girls and boys) coloured in red and blue. She put on her mittens and reindeer skin boots lined with grass, and she set off over the snow. The bright winter sun began to set in the clear blue sky. She knew the night would be bitterly cold, so she made towards the mountains looking for shelter. There she found a dark cave and ventured in for the night.

In the cave, in the darkness she felt a big warm furry animal fast asleep, so she lay down beside him and, exhausted, dropped into a deep slumber. As the days grew longer she woke up. What? She found herself lying next to a newly woken big brown bear staring at her.

He had become used to the smell of her in his long sleep, so he shared his berries, honey and nuts. Before long they fell in love and she became his wife. Never could she have wanted for a kinder husband and to add to her happiness they had a little boy child, very like a human boy except a little more hairy and with furry bear paws.

Each day the great bear would teach his wife and boy a little more about the plants of their wide open landscape called the Vidda. He showed them how every tree, every leaf, every flower and fruit could be used. Even moss and bark can be eaten or used as medicine if you know how and at last he had shared all his wisdom.

Then one day he said to his wife, 'I'm grown old. Now the hunters will kill me.'

'No!' she said. 'Don't speak like that. You have many good years left!'

'I'm sorry, my love,' said the bear. 'The hunters can sense that my power is weaker. Soon they will come and hunt me down. That's as it should be. I give myself freely. Tell them that you have been my wife. If they don't believe you, show them our child and ask for half of my meat. It will give you strength.'

Sure enough, a party of hunters climbed up to the cave and the great bear went out to meet them. He struck down the first hunter. That was the girl's oldest brother. Then the second came and the bear struck him down too. That was the girl's second brother. At last the youngest brother came and the old bear was killed by his spear.

The bear's body was taken down into the village and his wife came too with her child and told them the whole story. Her mother and father were amazed and welcomed her back into the warmth of the human family.

She and her boy lived there in contentment and shared the wisdom of the bear. They showed the other humans how every tree, every leaf, every flower and fruit has a different use, to be eaten, made into something or taken as medicine. The people learnt eagerly and so the practice of medicine was first discovered by the Sami people.

Hodja and His Donkey

Do you remember Hodja, the wise and at times silly man from Turkey? (Some people say his name is Nasruddin and he lives in Afghanistan or Iran.) Here is a story from when he was young.

When Hodja was a child, his dad had a fantastic job. He was the watchman for a great temple. He opened the grand temple gates in the morning, he kept the oil lamps burning brightly and then he sat around making sure that everything was alright. On their way out pilgrims put money in the pot and, since this was an important temple that they visited every year, Hodja's dad earned a lot of money. It was a brilliant job.

'Ah, little Hodja, when you are grown up you will inherit your father's job,' said the old women in the town. 'What a lucky boy!'

But when Hodja was fifteen years old he said, 'Father, I'm sorry, but I don't want your job when I grow up. I want to travel out into the world and search for the meaning of life.'

'Splendid!' said his father. 'Business is good. I will buy you a donkey.' So his father bought him a lovely little donkey at the market. Hodja packed his bag onto the donkey and was off.

Together they travelled far. Over Egypt, through Jerusalem and the Arabian deserts to Basra and Isfahan, travelling east, always east. Everywhere young Hodja spoke to wise people – monks, wise women, dervishes and even wise old trees. He asked them, 'What is the meaning of life?'

After many years of travelling, Hodja and his donkey came to the high mountains of the Hindu Kush. Struggling upwards on the steep path, suddenly the little donkey stumbled. Then, gasping in the thin air, it fell lifeless to the ground.

Hodja gasped in horror. His dear, faithful friend, who had followed him and helped him all these years, was gone. He buried the donkey under sand and rocks and fell weeping on the grave. At this point a large group of pilgrims were passing and they stopped and stared at him.

'This must be the place where a great holy saint has died,' they whispered. 'See how his faithful disciple cries out in sadness!'

One of the pilgrims happened to be a very rich man and when he saw the great sorrow of Hodja he called out, 'No, no! This cannot be tolerated! We must build in this very spot a mighty temple to remember this holy place!' At once he sent down to the nearest town for the best builders to start work on a colossal memorial.

Hodja was really embarrassed when he saw the work starting but he didn't know what to say, so he said nothing. For this reason the temple soon became known as 'The Temple of the Silent, Weeping Disciple'.

Rumours of the temple spread far and wide. It became very famous and at last came to the ears of Hodja's father himself. Hodja's father needed a holiday and decided to travel to this important temple. His nephew temporarily took over his job and he set off.

It was a long journey, but at last Hodja's father arrived. As he entered the dark temple, squinting from the daylight, he was most surprised to see his own son.

'Hodja, what on earth brings you here?' he asked.

Hodja said, 'Dear father, I'm so glad to see you! At last I can share my embarrassing secret. My beloved donkey, which you gave me, died right here. I fell down crying. At the same moment I realised the meaning of life – simply, love! But then people were convinced that I was crying over an important saintly teacher so they built this gigantic temple here. What shall I do? How can I tell them?"

At this his father threw his arms high into the air and called out, 'Glory be to God! Wonders will never cease! This was exactly how my temple started when my very own donkey died, nearly thirty years ago!'

Donkeys are amazing animals, in their natural state they are highly in-telligent. Unlike horses they are not herd animals. They like to think for themselves and their long ears reveal a keen sense of hearing. Perhaps it's not such a bad plan to build a temple to celebrate them.

Myths from the Land of You

Was there ever a time when you got really embarrassed? What did you do? Did you try to pretend nothing was wrong, like Hodja, or did you tell someone?

This next story is found in the Bible, the Koran, the Torah and in many other versions too. I once told it in a huge storytelling festival in Iran. It was the opening of the festival and a very important and serious-looking mullah got up in front of the crowd and said, 'You must never, EVER tell stories from the Koran except reading exactly the same words as it says in the book.' I had to tell next and this story is in the Koran but I knew I was going to tell it very differently. Was he going to get really angry with me and put me in prison, or what? But luckily the other Iranians that were there really liked my version. Some people tell a story exactly the same way they heard it, which I respect very much and it's awesome to think that some stories have been passed on like that for thousands of years.

The Ark

God cut into the darkness and let in the light. He trod down the earth and flung the heavens up into the air. He poured water into the oceans and into the water he threw the slippery slimy fish. He pulled up the mountains, covered them with forests and filled the forests and the air with creatures. It was good. So good! There was one creature God thought was particularly amazing. You should never have favourites among your children but still …

The Creator was busy. He was off doing things in other parts of the universe but when He got back and looked down He could not believe his eyes! What had happened? His favourites, those incredible human beings, had cut themselves off. They had built boxes around themselves and were separating themselves from the rest of creation. Maybe that's what happens when you get favourites? And He was just about to stamp on them when – he spied one family who were not lost. They were still totally connected. They had lots of animals and birds around their tents. They were laughing.

'Noah!' He called. Now this Noah was a big man. He had big hands, big knees, big ears. His wife used to say, 'You know why Noah has such big ears? He hears everything from the tiniest little ant right up to God.' When she said that, Noah laughed a big, echoing laugh.

That day Noah got a call from God. When he heard the call he said, 'I see, three hundred cubits. Yes, I'll get onto it right away. What? All of them? I'll do my best, Lord. I'll have to get help from the wife.'

That night Noah gathered his whole family round the fire and said, 'God had a word this morning. He has given me a big job. It's … I mean … BIG! If you don't want to help that's fine, but if you do, it will be hard work. But if we're able to do it, it will save not only us but all of the beautiful beasts, the creeping creatures and the birds too.'

'Yes,' they said. 'Yes. We want to help.'

So next day Noah went with his sons into the deep, dark, endless forest and they chopped and felled mighty trees. They harnessed horses and camels and donkeys and they dragged the trees into a great clearing.

They hacked, they chopped, they sawed.

They planed, they drilled, they carved.

They lifted, they carried, they pulled.

They hammered, they sanded, they polished.

They boiled great pans with sap which turned into steaming black pitch. They painted pitch on the inside and on the outside of the wood.

They had made a mighty monster ship. And they called it the Ark.

They made three decks in the Ark. They made big rooms for the big; they made tiny rooms for the tiny. Between the three decks were little ladders and corridors. The whole ship was like a mighty black labyrinth.

Meanwhile, do you think Mrs Noah, her sons' wives, Miriam, Mariam and Meriam, and her grandchildren were sitting back and watching the work? No! They were out cutting great bundles of grass, which they carried home on their heads. They were weaving sacks and filling them with corn and nuts. They had many animals and birds around their tents but Mrs Noah said it was not enough. They went out into the forests and the mountains to find two of every single kind, a male and a female. They made cages and nets and snares and they went looking for wild creatures that they had never seen before.

One day a boy came running up to Noah and said, 'Grandfather, we must collect all the animals. We can't leave any of them behind. But how can I catch a lion? Or a wolf, or a jackal? They will rip me to pieces and eat me.'

Noah laughed and lifted the boy up. The laugh was so big that the boy vibrated in his arms.

Early the next morning before the sun had risen, Noah walked up onto the mountain and into a dark cave. There, fast asleep, was a lion and a lioness. Noah had such a peace and certainty in his heart that the lions let him bind them and lead them down into the valley.

When did the first pub appear on the earth? You'll have to ask an archaeologist but they probably had pubs by the time of Noah. One day, down in the local pub, a rich landowner was drinking beer and he said to Noah's son, 'Japhet my lad! We haven't seen you in a long time. Now, look here. We think you should know that your dad Noah is completely bonkers. Why is he building a ship hundreds of miles away from the sea, not even near a lake? He is barking mad. No one has invented psychiatrists yet, so I suggest you leave home at once. I have a nice little job for you collecting rent.'

'No,' said Japhet. 'This is where you got him wrong. The reason my dad has such big ears is because he's listening. He's been trying to tell you a massive flood is coming but you don't take any notice.'

'Listen, Japhey,' said the pub owner. 'On a Saturday me and my family goes down your way, we takes a picnic and we 'as a good laugh. I mean, your old lady she's got a bloomin' zoo there, ain't she? You should be chargin' for that. You could be makin' tons of money!'

'Put it this way, Japhet,' shouted the rich landowner. 'Is anyone here in this pub making a boat? Any little rafts or even dinghies? No. You see, Japhet? Nobody else is making even a tiny boat. Now, statistically, think about it, how can your father be right and everyone else wrong? Eh?'

But the sky was darkening. Huge flocks of birds flew across the skies and the animals seemed restless. Noah's family made a heavy gangplank to the door of the Ark and carried baskets and chests filled with food. Down in the hold they put the large hippo, the great grey-skinned elephant, the rhino, the bison, the elk. All the heavyweights of creation were there and of each kind there was a bull and a cow. Then Noah led in the dangerous beasts – the wolf, the lion, the jaguar, the lynx, the great bears. Onto the middle deck they put the herd animals, the fast runners – the horse, donkey, wild pig, sheep and goat, the reindeer and the gazelle, a buck and a doe of every kind. Meanwhile the children ran back and forth, up and down the gangplank, carrying dogs, hedgehogs, cats, squirrels, monkeys, with cages of mice, rats, ferrets, snakes, frogs, toads, lemmings. On the topmost deck roosted the birds, from the tiniest wren and kingfisher up to the great swan, goose, eagle, peacock, albatross and emu. There were two of each kind of bird – the cock and the hen.

'Look up!' called Ham. Flying towards them was a cloud of butterflies, bees, wasps and other insects swarming. Even ants and spiders were creeping onto the Ark as if all they all understood.

The rain had begun to fall. 'Close the Ark!' called Noah, but as he did two children ran down the gangplank.

'Grandfather!' they said. The wind was blowing fiercely and they held fast to a tree as Noah joined them. 'Look, Grandfather,' and, sure enough, galloping across the valley was a herd of strange beasts he had never seen before, wet and bedraggled, two of each kind. Noah welcomed these exotic animals trembling onto the Ark. Then his three sons put their shoulders to the heavy door and slammed it tight.

Outside the Ark the thunder rumbled, the lightning crashed, the windows of heaven were opened and the rain poured down in torrents.

Inside the Ark the atmosphere was filled with fear. Soon tremendous noises rose of braying, bleating, barking and whinnying, mice squeaking, lions roaring and the birds screeching their piercing terrified calls. In the dark Noah reached out his hand to his wife and said, 'What a terrible sound. How will we bear it?'

My dearest,' Mrs Noah said, 'If not for this noise it would be worse. We would hear the cries of our neighbours drowning.'

After three days they felt a jolt and the Ark was lifted as if by a gentle but enormous hand. Noah and his three sons lit burning torches and searched high and low to see if water had come in, but the Ark was dry and safe. And it was floating. There was no motor, no sail or paddles to steer it as they moved out over the ocean.

As it moved, the big boat rocked from side to side like a giant baby's cradle and inside the creatures became calm and quiet. The rain fell outside, and a great peace descended in the Ark. Noah's family took it in turns to feed and care for the creatures. It rained for forty days and forty nights.

One day Mariam was up on deck emptying a bucket of emu manure into the sea when she looked up and saw a dazzling ribbon of silver lighting the horizon. 'Hey!' she called, 'Come up here!' It was the first glimpse of sun and the larks began singing.

What next? Noah let out the raven, which spread its wings and flew to the horizon. After seven days he released the dove into the sky. She flew around and back to the Ark again. Seven days later Noah set the dove free again. She returned with a tiny olive twig in her beak.

In the seventh month the Ark rested on Mount Ararat. They cracked open the great door and after all those months in the darkness everyone came out into the light. Some trotted or tripped nervously; others ran, skipped or flew. Some crawled, others gambolled out onto the earth. Many foals, kids and baby birds had been born during the long journey. And the family sat on the gangplank and watched them playing and frisking and the birds sang with all their might.

'Look up!' cried Noah and they saw a huge bow stretched across the skies in all the colours of light.

At that moment they knew that if they had to start from scratch and do it all again, they would.

Noah's Ark Quiz

1. What made God cross?
2. Was it just Noah and his sons who were helping?
3. How did Noah help his grandson?
4. How many of each kind of animal was in the ark?
5. How long did the rain fall?
6. What was in the bucket that Mariam was emptying?
7. What was the name of the mountain they landed on?

Myths from the Land of You

Take a famous story you really like – anything, a famous film or a fairytale, anything where you more or less remember the story. Tell it to yourself or a good friend and add lots of new details. If you do this with someone else you can take turns to retell the story with lots of extra descriptions.

Kikko

Stories are like animals, they come in all shapes and sizes – fat ones, thin snaky ones, ones the size of an ant. As you transform into a Natural Storyteller you will notice that people around you are telling stories, sometimes stories so great that you want to retell them, like this one my friend Zoe told me about her dog.

Kikko is a big, fuzzy lurcher dog. He is very obedient, follows Zoe around all day and never runs away.

Every now and then Zoe goes travelling and Kikko stays with Suzy, who lives on the other side of the village. Suzy can have up to eight dogs in her home. She takes them all out for a good walk twice a day, brushes them down and feeds them their various dinners. The dogs do as they are told and she is like the pack leader. After their morning walk, Suzy goes into her studio and makes lovely curtains for people. The dogs sit quietly on their own beds around the studio and wait till lunchtime and their afternoon walk.

One summer's day it had been a long time since Kikko had visited Suzy. Zoe was out in the orchard, which is surrounded by a high brick wall, when she suddenly noticed that Kikko had disappeared. Zoe looked everywhere. Kikko had never run off before and she couldn't for the life of her understand what had happened.

Finally there was a call from Suzy. Kikko had turned up at her house in the village. He must have jumped the high brick wall, crossed the busy road and found her.

'Zoe!' she said. 'How did Kikko know I needed him? One of the old dogs who has been coming here for years died this morning. I was so incredibly miserable and then Kikko came bouncing in to comfort me.'

They stayed with Suzy for an hour and then Zoe had to go back to work. That afternoon Zoe again let Kikko into the garden. She watched this time and, sure enough, Kikko walked down the long garden path, every now and then looking back at her. It was as if he was saying, 'I'm going.' Sure enough he got to the wall, looked back once more, then clambered over it and shot up the drive out of sight.

Zoe got into the car and drove over to Suzy. Sure enough, there he was again! This time she took Suzy out for a walk and invited her over for supper.

Kikko has never run off before or since. It was just twice on that day. Somehow from the other side of the village he knew Suzy was feeling sad and needed him.

Before you move on to the next story, take a moment to dream a little. Sit back, relax in yourself and watch the story of Kikko in your mind. Do you remember the whole thing?

Take a deep breath. The last story in Story Animal *is a biggie. Not a beginner's story. If you do want to tell it, here is a tip: work on it hard using any of the tricks you have learnt like story map, story skeleton, shutting your eyes and seeing it like a film, making a quiz or a map outside. When you finally tell it to someone else, tell it as if you were telling about your friend's dog. Don't march importantly about as if you are the chief storyteller at King Arthur's court. Tell it as yourself – you are your own best storyteller.*

King of the Deer

Beneath the mountains of the Himalayas was a mighty forest. In a thicket of this forest a mother doe hid from the wild beasts and gave birth to her baby fawn. Here she cleaned him gently and tenderly until he sprang up. Like every newborn fawn, he could already run faster than the swiftest of Olympic athletes. But he didn't run, he stood quite still looking about him with eyes twinkling like diamonds. His coat was soft and golden, his small antlers were silver, his hooves gleaming jet black. As he pranced about his hooves struck the rocks making showers of sparks. Then he and his mother ran together with the herd. This little fawn grew up fast and became a mighty powerful stag, King of the Deer.

This whole huge forest teemed with life. There were bears, lions, monkeys, buffalo and countless other animals. The skies were full of birds and the rivers teemed with fish. No creature in that forest was alone; each one was an atom of the whole. Like a tree where every leaf, every branch or root plays its part. In the forest there were also people, gathering wood and nuts, and beside it in the city lived their king, King Brahmadatta.

King Brahmadatta was very clever. He had learnt science, music and art. He had trained with the best archers, the finest horsemen. But there was one thing he loved: he was crazy about hunting. Every day he rode out with a large band of hunters. Every day blood was spilled, splashing the earth red, and every evening wagons returned to the palace, piled high with the bodies of dead animals. The hunters rode over farmlands, trampling crops and scattering cattle.

One day the prime minister summoned all his courage and told the king, 'Your Majesty, your people are so angry with your hunting that they refuse to pay their taxes.' So, reluctantly, King Brahmadatta agreed to a plan. Part of the forest was fenced off and he promised to hunt only there.

The King had a tall tower built and each morning the huntsmen beat the deer out into the open and he climbed the tower to shoot at them. Already that first morning he saw a great stag he had never seen before. 'Stop!' he called to his men, 'Look, this stag is like me. He is a king among his kind. He must be spared. Never harm a hair on his body.'

Every day the huntsmen came and the bloodshed was terrible. The deer were terrified, many died from the metal-tipped arrows, and others got trapped in the fence and trampled one another to death in their fear. The King of the Deer found the destruction of his people horrible to see. He asked his mother, the old doe, for advice, and she said, 'Listen, son, I have a plan. We will make a lottery. Each day one of our people will be chosen, a willing sacrifice, and the others will be spared.'

It was agreed and the next day one trembling buck came out into the killing fields, bowing its head. For the first time King Brahmadatta glimpsed the intelligence of the deer. 'Look, this buck is offering himself so the others can live. Such wisdom! Shoot only him.' But this was no sport and the king put down his bow and returned to the palace. From that time only one deer was killed each day.

One morning, as the dawn rose pink and the birds were singing their sunrise symphony, the King of the Deer was browsing peacefully with his people when a young doe came running towards him. She bowed her head and said, 'Your Majesty, the lottery has fallen to me this day, and I will gladly bear it, but please not now. There is an unborn fawn inside me.'

'Our law demands one life not two,' said the King. 'You are spared.'

'But who will go in my place?' she asked.

'Don't worry,' said the King of the Deer. 'I will see to it.'

But as the golden beams of sun shone down amongst the leaves the King watched his people quietly grazing and he could not lay the burden onto another. So that morning he himself walked slowly out of the forest. The hunters in the tower saw his silver antlers gleaming, his coat golden. He stood still and solid, no fear or tremble in his strong form, and the hunters knew this was the animal the king had told them never to shoot. They sent a message. Soon they heard galloping hooves. The king climbed the tower and called down, 'Great stag! Don't you see, we will not shoot you? Why are you standing here?'

To his astonishment the stag lifted his head and replied: 'This morning a doe carrying a fawn in her belly asked for my mercy. Our lottery calls for one life, not two. So I came myself.'

'So you are King of the Deer! This was a noble act. A true king cares for all his people, even the weakest. For this I decree that all your deer will be released from the fence and can run free in the forest.'

'Thanks, oh King, for your great gift, but I cannot accept it.'

'What do you mean? Don't be stupid! Do you want your people to die?'

'Your Majesty,' said the King of the Deer. 'If we are saved, what about the other animals? How can we go free, knowing that they will be hounded and hunted all the more? I cannot buy our freedom at such a price.'

'This is too much,' blurted King Brahmadatta. 'You are going beyond your duty now.'

'No, king of men. The tiger, the elephant, the monkeys, the boars, they are our sisters and brothers. If we are free their suffering is doubled.'

The human king felt himself blushing with both shame and admiration at the kindness of this beast.

'Yes, very well, perhaps you are right. Then I promise to free all the animals from the danger of the hunt. So! Now you may go in peace.'

The stag stood still, steady as a rock. 'Your Majesty, I cannot accept your offer.'

King Brahmadatta was stunned. 'What do you mean? I have just agreed to stop hunting all the animals in the forest!'

'Yes King, but what about all the birds of the air, all the fishes of the rivers? Each and every one has, like you and me, white bones to hold them upright. Each one has eyes to see and ears to hear. Every one is covered with skin, like us, though some sprout feathers, some fur and some fins. Each one is blessed with an intricate brain, like ours, divided into the left and the right. And each and every one has a beating heart that warms with love for their young. No. I cannot buy my life to see your hooks, your spears and arrows bring their suffering.'

The king stared at the deer. Tears were pouring down his face.

'Great being,' he said, 'why have I never seen this before? Today I will send out a decree. No one in my kingdom may hunt the birds, animals or fishes. Are you satisfied now, my teacher?'

'Yes!' said the King of the Deer. And he threw back his head and jumped high in the air. Such was his joy. His coat shone like burnished gold, his crown of antlers like silver and as he landed his jet black hooves sent up a shower of sparks. He turned once more to look at King Brahmadatta with his diamond gaze and said, 'Yes, now I will go. Thank you.'

The King called for his hunters to start taking down the fence. Then he stood watching as the deer went their ways, threading their paths into the forest.

King Brahmadatta became a wise and much beloved king. At first his people found it hard to stop eating meat, but from that day a delicious vegetarian cuisine grew up in India. And when the king was old he went to the spot where he had met the deer and began to cut into a large stone. He chipped away to make a statue of a stag. And beneath it stood these words: 'Here, in this place, I found my teacher. Here a deer taught King Brahmadatta to become a better man.'

The King of the Deer also lived to a good old age. When he died, which stag do you think became the next king? The same fawn whose life he had saved while it lay, still unborn, in its mother.

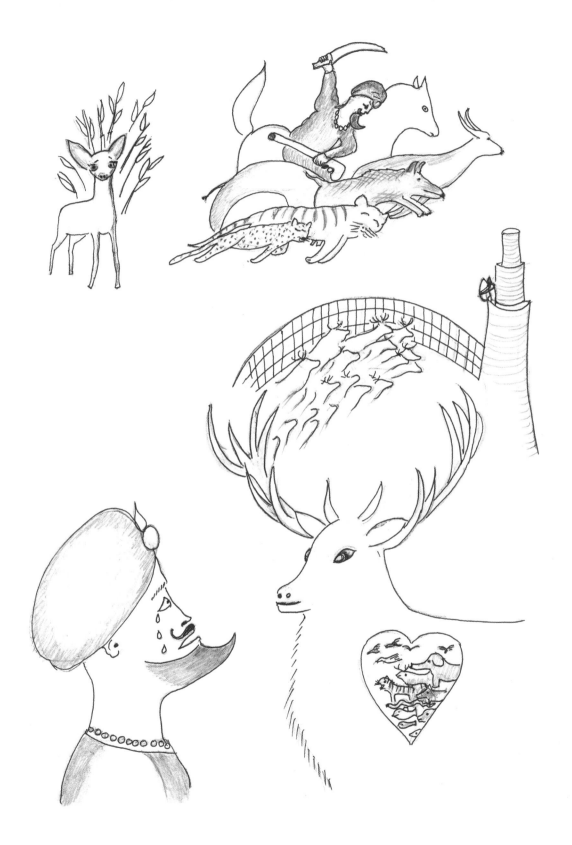

In *Story Animal* you have met many animals and the people who knew them. Here is a new task for you as you tread the trail towards becoming a *Natural Storyteller* ...

Getting closer to wild animals is not easy. Wild animals can be shy of us humans, and who can blame them? Some people even shoot tiny birds to eat. But wild animals and birds are often very curious about us too.

Here is a game to learn how to track; it's a game for two or many players.

Deer Tracker's Game

1. Go to a forest or a beach or somewhere you can see tracks on the ground.
2. Find a nice log or stone that's heavy but not too heavy to drag.
3. Attach a rope to it.
4. Choose one person to be the deer.
5. Everyone else gets in a scrum with their arms round each other and sings so that the deer can't be heard.
6. Then the deer very quietly starts dragging the log and making a trail.
7. After some time everyone follows the tracks and sees if they can find their deer friend.

Tracking Wildlife

There may be many wild creatures near where you live or by your school. Perhaps you can discover some telltale signs they have left. Can you spot one of the following clues?

TRACKS
To find tracks is easiest if you are lucky enough to have a fall of snow, or if there

is some mud or dust where you can see the tracks clearly. A dog, mouse, deer, bird or even an insect leaves tracks. If you leave some suitable food out probably someone will eat it. Check the tracks and see if you can tell who it is.

PINE CONE CLUES

There are probably squirrels living not too far away from where you live. If you live near the woods you can check the pine cones. Squirrels have a special way of eating the cones which is different from the way woodpeckers or mice eat. They also eat nuts and seeds and are the greatest tree planters in the whole world, as they love to bury nuts. See if you can find some pine cones or pine nut shells which have been nibbled at.

BURROWS AND NESTS

Foxes, mice, rabbits and many other animals dig themselves a hole to live in. See if you can spot at least one animal home dug in the ground. If you see a lot of large holes you may have stumbled on a badger set. Some people go on a badger safari at night. Badgers are big shy animals, but, like anyone else, if they get scared and cornered they can bite, so it's good to keep a bit of distance. Go with a sensible grown-up and bring a thermos of cocoa and lots of warm clothes. Wait patiently and maybe you will be lucky.

SCAT

Last but not least, one of the best ways to track which wild beasts live in your neighborhood is to check their poo; the professional tracker word for this is 'scat'. Each has their own distinctive shape. In my local forest we find beautiful beads – elk poo has such a perfect shape you can drill a little hole in them and make a necklace!

If you go out tracking, you will experience something that will help you to tell stories about animals, that will make your stories more realistic and true. Even if you don't find any traces you will find out how it is to be an animal looking for another animal.

Did you find the answer to the two riddles at the start of *Story Animal*?

The answers are animals from two different parts of the earth. Here they are again:

1. I jump when I walk and I sit where I stand. What am I?

2. You are standing very near to a mammal. You walk one kilometre to the south. Then you walk one kilometre to the west. Then you walk one kilometre due north. Oh my goodness, you are back next to the same animal. Which animal is it?

Number one is a kangaroo. Number two: if you walk first south, then west, then north to get back to the same place, you are at the North Pole, so it has to be a polar bear.

Story Bird

As a *Natural Storyteller* you will also need to learn to fly. Not an easy task but if you manage it, it will happen without even leaving the ground.

No one is saying it's simple but then being a *Natural Storyteller* is a bit like having magical powers. As you tell a story you need to see it so crystal clear in your mind, it´s almost like you are there. When you do that, then the listeners will see it too.

How do you get the story into your mind? Relax your body, shut your eyes and watch it as if you are seeing it in a film or are actually there. For example if there is a bird in your story you see every feather ruffling in the breeze, and its twinkling eyes and sharp beak. Perhaps the bird is perched high on a rock with a sweet breeze blowing up from the valley. Then, when you see the bird clearly, imagine you ARE it. Ruffle your feathers and twitch your wings; gaze out through your powerful eyes. What do you see at the bottom of the valley?

Now choose a story you like from this book and read through it once. Choose a really cosy place to be and see the whole story in your mind. Don't tell the story to yourself in words; just see it or feel as if you are there, or as if you are seeing a film in your mind. It can be such a nice feeling to do this. You may find hidden corners in the story that you didn´t know were there. It will probably start to change a bit and become your own story.

But don´t rush out and tell it to a massive football stadium full of people yet! Walk around and tell it to yourself once or twice. Then tell it to your dad or a tree or anyone else who is patient and good at listening. It may start to come to life and once it has hatched out, it's yours ...

Back to the flying training. As flying is hard, this is an extra hard riddle. Super fiendishly tricky. I'll be amazed if you guess it. If you don't you will find the answer at the end of the section.

In marble walls as white as milk,

Lined with a skin as soft as silk,

Within a fountain crystal clear,

A golden apple doth appear.

No doors there are to this stronghold,

Yet thieves break in and steal the gold.

Story Bird will help you imagine what it's like to be a bird. Some of the stories are from history; others are from mythology.

The Puffin

Two hundred years ago, a mother and a father puffin stood atop a steep mountain island in Norway. These two puffins had lived together for twenty years, for puffins are faithful birds. They were looking out over the sea with their orange beaks, white faces and black dinner jacket suits. They had big orange feet and looked a bit like two small clowns but they were not clowns, they were puffins.

High up on the cliff, they had cut the earth with their beaks, cleared it out with their feet and made a long burrow. That day, the mother puffin trundled along to the end of the burrow. There in the dark, she laid an egg and sat on it to keep it warm.

Forty days later in the darkness the mother and father heard a cracking sound. Then there was a little tweeting noise and they knew a new chick had been born. They took it in turns to stretch their wing over the chick and keep him warm. For seven weeks the chick waited in the darkness as his parents flew back and forth to find food. Often they had to fly far and dive deep under the sea to find the right fish. Then they carried about ten small herrings in their beaks back to their chick deep in the burrow.

Seven weeks later the young puffin began to toddle along. As he reached the mouth of the tunnel at the top of the cliff he saw all the other young puffins. They were also standing in their tunnels with no space to flutter and hop and test their wings. But on this day the other little puffins were jumping and he knew he too must launch himself into the world. So our puffin chick flung himself out from the high cliff and plunged down towards the water.

When he reached the surface of the water he dived down. Once under the sea he was safe from hungry ravens, eagles and gulls. There were thousands of puffins large and small here in the water that day. Now our young puffin had another test. In the darkness of the burrow he had hardly seen his mother and father but now he listened. From amongst the banter of the thousand birds he heard their voices and found his own mum and dad. They taught him to fly, to dive and to fish.

This bird mountain stood on a little island where a fisherman lived. The fisherman was tall, broad-shouldered and handsome. He loved his island and he wanted someone to share his life there. So one day he rowed his boat over to the mainland to find himself a wife. There, in a little farm, he found a girl. She could milk a cow, clean fish, bake bread, brew beer and do a hundred other jobs and he fell madly in love and asked her to marry him. What the young fisherman didn't know was that whenever he turned to leave her, his heart beating and happy, the girl's sister whispered to her, 'Do you know where that fisherman comes from? He comes from Røst. Those miserable islands without a single tree! If you go out there over the stormy sea you'll be his slave. It will be nothing but hard work and starvation.' But it was too late. The girl had given her heart already and she took her little wooden chest with all her worldly belongings, jumped into his fishing boat and was gone.

A full year later the older sister came to visit. From the moment she stepped onshore her mouth was hanging open. She saw birds of all colours and shapes, underground stores filled with hundreds of bird eggs, and great barrels of salted fish of many sizes and flavours. She stared at the rich earth where the vegetables seemed to burst out of the ground. Because of the Gulf Stream there was a mild winter, a generous harvest and both cows and sheep grazing in the meadow. Her sister looked so happy and was carrying a beautiful baby on her arm. Even the fisherman seemed twice as handsome as he had been the year before.

Perhaps you think she was happy that her sister had found such a nice place to live. No. As meals were laid out on the table, each one more tasty and lavish than the last, a stinging jealously burnt ever deeper into her heart.

One bright midsummer night, she was sleepless and shivering. Every time she tried to sleep a sharp envious thought woke her. The night was warm, but she was cold and she got up to kindle a fire in the hearth. Suddenly she leant towards the fire, took out a burning stick, ran outside and began to clamber up the steep mountain, past birds quietly sleeping in their nests. When she reached the top, there among the rocks who did she see sitting and warming himself in the midnight sun?

It was our friend the young puffin. Now he was five years old, fully grown, plump and ready to find himself a mate. Then the sister did a terrible thing. It's hard to know why. Maybe the little puffin, glossy and happy, reminded her of her sister? She seized him by the neck, took the burning stick and set light to his flapping wings. As the fire caught the feathers the sister spat words of hate out into the night air. Evil poured from her mouth as the smoke billowed and the bird's cries of pain echoed around the mountain. In their thousands the other birds awoke.

Below, the fisherman jumped up and came out to see what the noise was and why the sky was dark with birds. Then, as if there was one thought in all the hearts of all the birds, they all flew away in a cloud of feathers.

'Why? Why did you do it?' called the fisherman to the sister.

'Because life is so unfair. You have everything and I have nothing.'

'Dear sister,' said the fisherman. 'Here on this island there is more than enough for all of us. Even if the birds never come back.'

They say that the sister repented of the horrible thing she had done, and she found the good life on the many islands of Røst. But on that particular bird mountain the birds never came back, except for the occasional sea eagle looking for food.

A few years back I was walking in North Norway and met Kari, who lives on the islands of Røst. She pointed to the bird mountain in this story where there were no birds at all. She told me the story which tells why there are no birds there now. The next day I met an ornithologist. That word sounds a bit off-putting, but in actual fact he has a very thrilling job. He studies birds. Ornithologists discover things like bird language, how birds talk to each other, how they navigate over thousands of miles, how they are related to dinosaurs, etc. He told me about the fantastic life of puffins and how he is working to protect them. Birds are hundreds of times better than us at lots of things. Millions of times better at flying. The Natural Storyteller gets to know some of these secrets. When you tell a story you can have a lot of fun doing research, i.e. finding out about the bird in your story, or the person or the place.

The Blind Little Sister

In a village in West Africa, two sisters lived happily together. Then the older sister fell in love and married a hunter. A hunter with no time for the younger sister. He said she was no use because she was blind.

Each day he stormed into the forest with traps and spears and when he came back the blind sister said, 'I would love to go hunting one day.

The hunter stared at her, shaking his head violently. 'I should think not! What use is a hunter with no eyes? And on top of that you are a girl.'

Then his wife would say quietly, 'My sister is the wisest person I know. She sees with her ears.'

It was the same every evening. The blind sister asked, 'Please let me come hunting tomorrow.' All the while the hunter became more and more angry.

One evening the hunter dragged home a fat gazelle which the sisters prepared with delicious spices. He was in such a good mood, he said, 'All right, tomorrow you can come. But just this once and don't get in my way!'

The next day the hunter led the blind girl by the hand. They walked in silence but suddenly the blind girl stopped.

'Shhhh, there is a lion!' The hunter stared at the lush trees and pretty birds but he couldn't see any lion. 'Not to worry,' said the blind girl. 'The lion has eaten and he's fast asleep. He won't hurt us.'

A few moments later, sure enough, they came upon a mighty lion stretched out like a huge sleepy cat under a tree. As soon as they had passed, the hunter whispered, 'How in the world did you know about that lion?'

'Oh, it's easy. I see with my ears,' said the girl.

Further into the jungle again the girl gripped his hand. 'Shhh,' she whispered, 'an elephant!' Again the hunter stared feverishly around but saw absolutely nothing but creepers and flowering trees. Then the girl said, 'Ah, not to worry, the elephant is happily washing. He won't bother us.'

A little further on, sure enough, a great bull elephant was wallowing and splashing in a water hole. 'How on earth did you know about that elephant?' asked the hunter.

'It's simple, I see with my ears,' said the sister.

They continued on until they came to a sunlit clearing and the hunter said, 'Let's each set a trap and we'll come back tomorrow to see what we have caught.'

Early next morning the hunter offered to hold the girl's hand but she said, 'It's OK, I know the way now.' Sure enough, she walked quietly along the path without stumbling.

At last they reached the sunlit clearing. The hunter saw at once there was a little grey bird in his trap. In the blind girl's trap was a bird that sparkled with feathers of scarlet and gold.

'Have a rest,' he said. 'We have both caught a bird.' As he went towards the traps he thought, 'A girl with no eyes will never know the difference.' And what did he do? He gave the girl the little grey bird and kept the scarlet bird for himself.

The girl took the little grey bird gently in her hands and they set off home. It was so quiet walking together the hunter started thinking. Suddenly he said, 'My wife is always saying how wise you are. If it's true then tell me the answer to this question that bothers me: why is there so much war and violence in this world?'

The blind girl answered softly, 'Because the world is full of people like you – who take things that are not theirs.'

The hunter stopped in his tracks, suddenly filled with bitter shame. He took the little grey bird from the girl's hands and gave her the sparkling scarlet and golden bird.

'I'm sorry,' he said.

For a long time again they walked in silence and then the hunter said, 'If you are so wise, please tell me one more thing. It's true, people are selfish, but how is it there is still so much love and kindness in the world?'

The girl smiled and said, 'Because the world is full of people like you, people who learn by their mistakes.'

From that day on if the hunter heard anyone ask, 'Blind girl, how is it you are so wise?' he would put an arm around her shoulder and say, 'I'll tell you. Because she sees with her ears and hears with her heart.'

In Africa and all over the world people tell stories to make us think deeply. If you decide to tell this story, you might wait in silence for a few moments at the end so it gets time to sink in.

Francis of Assisi

Did you ever try to speak, sing or whistle to a bird? Sometimes they do answer. This story is about someone who talked directly to birds.

In the centre of Italy lies a town called Assisi. Assisi stands atop a hill, like a crown. Hundreds of years back in time, in a grand house of Assisi lived a rich merchant and his wife. The merchant often travelled abroad to buy gorgeous fabrics, so he was not at home when his wife gave birth to their first baby.

A few days later there was a tremendous knocking and shouting at the door. The new mother came down to see what the rumpus was about and saw a rough and dirty traveller. 'I'll ask the cook to fetch you food,' she said.

'I don't want food, Madonna!' he answered. 'Just let me hold your chick for a moment.' Something kind in the eyes of the tattered man persuaded her to agree. So she passed him the precious bundle and he lifted the baby high in the air and said, 'Madonna, take good care of your baby bird. If he grows up he will fly – he will be one of the best people the world has ever known, one who loves the whole of creation.'

The new mother said her little Francis began to dance before he could walk. She said he started singing before he could talk. As he grew older she would often find him up in a tree singing like a happy little bird.

At the age of eleven he began work in his father's shop and his dad was proud of him as he charmed money out of the customers' pockets. As he grew older, his dad bought Francis a lute – like a small guitar – and he learnt fast and soon jumped onto a table in the pub and sang like a nightingale. After work he and his rich friends loved to ride their horses into the forest. They bought fancy new swords and practised fighting.

Then one day war broke out and they prepared for battle. As they cantered on their fine horses they sang and boasted about how famous, daring and heroic they would be.

On the battlefield, Francis was one of the last to arrive. There was chaos on every side and on the ground lay someone in a suit of newly polished armour. The pale face of Massimo called to him: 'Francis!' It was too late; Francis jumped down to his side but was powerless as his friend's life poured out with his blood. Francis was taken prisoner. For a whole year he was locked in darkness, until his father sent a large ransom and he made the long journey home.

When he got back to Assisi, he no longer saw the point of working in his father's shop. Instead he wandered all day alone in the forest. One evening a bunch of his friends came round. 'What's up, Francis? Why don't you come out and party with us anymore? Have you found a secret girlfriend?'

'Yes,' he said, 'she is beautiful.'

'What?' they said. 'What's her name? Where does she live?'

'She lives in the forest and her name is ... Nothing.' His friends stared at Francis. They shook their heads and said to each other, 'Poor Francis, what a weirdo he turned out to be.'

That night Francis sat at dinner staring at his plate. His father urged him to eat and he blurted out, 'Dad! I feel sick seeing all this food. Don't you realise there are people in Assisi who are starving? What's the point of all this? Does it make us happy? Look at the birds – they only take what they need. Why are we so greedy?'

The next day his father went away. Francis entered the shop and piled bales of expensive fabric onto his horse. He rode to the next town, sold the fabric and his valuable horse. With the money he bought food and clothes for those who were hungry and cold. Assisi is a small town and it didn't take long before his father heard about it and was absolutely furious.

The rich merchant went storming to the bishop, demanding that his son be put on trial and punished. Trials were held in the public marketplace and when people heard that the merchant was taking his own son to court they crowded into the square. A scandal not to be missed!

Red faced and angry, the merchant stood up and told the town how his son had stolen from his shop. On the cathedral steps the bishop said, 'Francis, you've heard your father. I know you have given to the poor and sick. But don't you understand? Stealing from your own father to feed the poor still makes you a thief.'

Francis bowed his head. 'Father, I have stolen from you and that was wrong. I can never repay you all that you have given me. But I will give you what I have.' He gave his father a leather purse filled with money and then, in front of the crowds, he took off his fine velvet cloak and gave it to his father. He took off his silken shirt and leather boots. He took off all his clothes and gave them to his father until he stood completely naked! Everyone was staring wide-eyed. Francis said, 'A father who cares more about money than love is no father for me. From now on my father is God in heaven.' Then he took an old worn cloak from the bishop and disappeared off into the forest.

From that day Francis lived in the forest without money. He prayed and helped the poor and the sick. He began to sing again. First a few friends came and asked if they could join him. He said yes but if they wanted to live there they had to give away all their money. As time went on, people flocked to join him in their thousands.

One summer's day a crowd had gathered on a path by the forest to hear Francis speak. 'Good morning!' he said. 'Friends, we are part of a huge family of living things. All of them are our brothers and sisters. Brother Sun warms us and lights our way. Sister Earth feeds us. Brother Wind cools us. Sister Water quenches our thirst.' As he spoke Francis noticed many birds hovering and flying around. There were doves, sparrows, crows and many others. Francis left his friends in the road and joined the birds. He greeted them and bowed, half-expecting them to fly off as he spoke. But they seemed to be waiting for him.

Filled with awe, he said, 'Brothers and sisters, what glorious feathers you are wearing. Your dazzling wings remind me of angels I have dreamt of. Your homes are the purest and freshest I have seen. Without farming, sowing or reaping, you harvest food from everything growing. Let's rejoice together at all that we are given completely free every single day?'

Hearing this the birds began to spread their wings, stretch their necks and open their beaks, singing and thanking God in their own bird languages. Francis then walked towards them touching their heads and bodies with his tunic.

Later, Francis wondered why he had never done this before. And from that day on, he made it his habit to pray with all birds, animals and reptiles.

True or False?

1. Francis was born in Assisi in Scotland.
2. His dad was a miserable tattered beggar.
3. When he was eleven years old Francis had to go out to work.
4. He loved playing war.
5. Francis was best friends with a Scottish bag piper.
6. His dad took him to court for stealing.
7. He said nature was in the same family as us.

Myths from the Land of You

Have you ever heard of someone who lived outside in the forest like Francis? What would that be like? Imagine a summer's night, stars instead of a roof, the soft forest floor, bracken for a mattress, hearing the squirrels and the birds waking you early in the morning.

Best Friends

A few years ago I went out walking by myself for seven weeks up in the north of Norway. I took a hammock with me. My plan was to sleep in the hammock between the trees. As I had never slept alone outside before I didn't know if I would dare to do it or be scared stiff and go to a hotel.

I wanted to collect stories about the connection between people and nature. However I was very unsure if I would be brave enough to go up to complete strangers with that question, but somehow I did. It was a fantastic journey.

Most people said to me, 'Sorry, I don't know any stories. Ask in the library, ask in the museum or maybe ask my neighbour.' But then we kept on chatting and in the end it turned out that every single person had a story. I heard loads of incredible tales. Very many of the stories were about people making friends with birds, like Clare Kipps in London.

During the Second World War a baby sparrow chick fell out of its nest. A passer-by scooped it up and put it on a nearby doorstep. The doorstep belonged to Clare Kipps, who opened her door that day and, finding this scrap of life, took it in. She began to feed it two drops of warm milk every hour. The tiny chick survived but one of his wings was broken. So Clare found a twig and tied up his wing in a splint. It got better but he was never that good at flying.

The sparrow made a little nest in her bed and from that first day he always kept the nest spotlessly clean. Some weeks later, Clare lent her bed to a friend and there was a terrible scene. The little bird ran up and down the pillow, scolding and then attacking the friend so she had to get out of bed and wait patiently while the sparrow got comfortable. This friend was a doctor and she had experienced many strange things but had never been ordered out of bed by a sparrow before.

As the sparrow was handicapped, Clare didn't think it would survive in the wild, so it lived in her bungalow. Clare was a widow who lived alone and every day she played with the sparrow. She bought him a cage, as she was worried she might step on him, but she always left the door open. The little sparrow used her legs as if they were tree trunks, her fingers as perches, fluttered around as if he was having a dust-bath on her head and liked to swing on her curly hair. Not only that, he began to do all sorts of tricks.

In September that year the bombing of London began in earnest. Clare worked as an air raid warden. During bombing raids by the Nazis she had to make sure everyone went into air raid shelters. Towards the end of the month when she was out working a bomb fell on her bungalow. When she got back the whole place was wrecked and she ran into the room where she had left the cage, calling out, 'Are you alive?' A little voice replied at once and, when the smoke had cleared, she saw the sparrow sitting calmly on his swing. The roof of the cage had caved in, a brick lay on it within an inch of his head and the floor was thick with broken glass. By chance or instinct he had taken refuge on his swing which had kept him safe from the blast.

In her work around London, Clare had to comfort many people. In those days there was no television and very little entertainment so she got an idea. She started to take the little sparrow round to show his tricks to soldiers and cheer them up. No bird ever served his country as faithfully as the sparrow did in those terrible months. People who had lost their homes and all their possessions forgot their troubles at least for a time. Terrified children became merry and carefree. Some who had refused to allow their gas masks to be tried on held up their head if promised a game with the sparrow. Even in houses where people refused to let Clare in, the doors were opened with a smile if the young sparrow arrived.

But what were his tricks? He would sit on his favourite pudding-basin and people from the audience fed him hemp seeds. Then he would leap out. As if he was transforming himself into Superman he had a tug of war against Clare using a hairpin. He held it fiercely in his beak – pulling with all his might until he won and carried off the hairpin trophy in triumph. Then he would pick a card chosen by the audience and turn it around with his beak. His most popular performance was the 'Air-Raid-Shelter Trick'. Clare called out, 'Siren's gone, bombs coming, run for shelter!' and he would run into her hands and stay in there quietly for several minutes. Finally he poked out his head as if asking if it was safe now.

After her bungalow had been bombed she had to move into another house. The other people in the house had a cat, which loved glaring into the cage. So Clare left the sparrow in a locked room but she worried he would get bored. However one day she listened outside the door and heard an extraordinary sound. A strange little song that began with a twittering, then a melody and a high note, far above the usual note of a sparrow and then, wonder of wonders, a little trill. After that the sparrow practised his song every day. This was the first time anyone had heard of a sparrow making such music and Clare decided to hold a concert. An audience came, he performed beautifully but at the end the clapping so terrified him that he disappeared down into the neck of her jumper and never sang for a human audience again.

When they moved back into the bungalow, he sang pretty much every day. Then all the wild birds of the neighbourhood would fly to his window and stand there staring and jostling each other as if frantically discussing his talents. His main fans were sparrows, blue tits and an occasional robin. Clare usually left the window open so they could fly in. One little blue tit in particular haunted his window from dawn to dusk and seemed terribly in love with him. But perhaps the sparrow's only love was Clare. He showed no interest in the other birds.

Usually sparrows don't live more than four years but he reached twelve years of age! All his long life he kept learning new things and keeping Clare entertained. When he had grown very old and weak and lost all his feathers she thought he was going to die. A vet prescribed champagne and, sure enough, she gave him a teaspoon twice a day for a fortnight and he was completely restored. He was nearly blind but his hearing was still acute and he lived for one more year. On his last day he settled himself quietly in her warm hand and lay motionless for some hours. Suddenly he lifted his head, called to her in his old friendly way and was gone.

Myths from the Land of You

Did you ever meet an animal or bird who you would like to be your friend? Would you like them to sleep in your bed and follow you around everywhere? If you tell this story you could make up some adventures that happened when they started speaking to you.

The Hoopoe's Story

Long ago there were such troubles in the world that a group of birds decided to find the wise and mighty bird, the Simurgh, to ask for help.

It was a long journey to the Simurgh. Flying over a great desert the little sparrow was beating its wings frantically, thinking, 'I will never keep up with the other birds.' Despite its fear, it didn't give up and all of a sudden it had caught up with the beautiful and glamorous hoopoe.

'Excuse me,' said the little sparrow, 'I hope you don't think I'm being cheeky but I can't help wondering where you got your beautiful golden crown of feathers?'

'Oh yes, I will tell you!' said the hoopoe. 'It's always good to have a story to shorten the way. And it's a good one. This story has been passed on by song of beak for many generations.

'Once, a great flock of my birds, the hoopoes, were flying over just such a desert as this. They looked down and saw a man lying on the ground. Now, as you know, we birds can see the energy radiating out of all creatures and there was a tremendous force field vibrating around this man, though he lay unconscious on the sand.

'So my ancestors, the hoopoes, flew down and hovering over him they shaded him from the sun. Feeling the sudden protection, the man awoke and gazed up to see a living parasol of birds hovering above him. He stood up, bowed reverently to the birds and began to walk back over the desert to his palace. This man was none other than the famous King Solomon himself.

'Now in those times the humans kept messenger birds, usually doves, and before long a dove was sent to my people from Solomon inviting them to a feast. On the appointed day, they arrived and were very impressed by the feast. Solomon's servants had found the fattest worms and juiciest beetles for them to eat and when the feast was over he said, "My friends, you saved my life. Tell me what I can give you as thanks? Ask for anything and it will be yours."

'The birds looked at his golden crown. Then they called out, all together, "Oh

Solomon, we adore your shining headdress. Please give us a crown like yours."

'"Certainly!" he cried and he sent for his finest goldsmiths. Tiny crowns were fitted for each and every one of them. They were delighted. From that time we have all had crowns. But my friend, I see the desert is coming to an end. Let's go down and rest for the night in those trees ...'

So the sparrow was strengthened by the hoopoe's story and managed to fly the long journey to the great wise Simurgh. But that's another story....

Myths from the Land of You

What happened when you woke up and found you had turned into a sparrow ...

The Bashak

If you are not sure which story to tell, it can be nice to choose a story from a place where someone or their mum and dad has come from. This next massive tale is from Iraq. Usually when Iraq is in the news they tell us something sad or scary, not what an amazing country it is. Once after this long story there were a lot of hands up and a boy said proudly, 'I am from Iraq!' He told us that he had once drunk a sip of 'the Water of Life' from this story. The water had been brought in a bottle to Norway from the lake in Iraq.

In the ancient land of Iraq many wonders have been seen. There once lived a hunter who caught birds of all sizes and colours to sell in the marketplace. He and his wife had a son who they loved more than all the world. One day the hunter called his son and said, 'My child, as you know, your mother and I cannot read or write. But I have saved money so that you can go to school.'

The boy went to school and studied well. When he came home each afternoon his father would give him a little pet bird, butterfly or animal. In the evening he would read aloud thrilling stories and beautiful poetry for his parents. Many years passed in happiness together. One afternoon when he returned from school his father was not there. So he set off, up hill and down dale. As he walked he called out, 'Dad! Where are you? Dad!' But there was no reply.

At last, up in the high mountains, he saw his father's cloak and spear lying beside a terrifying steep drop. He peered over the edge of the cliff and saw his fathers' body lying lifeless far below. Already animals and birds were gnawing on his bones. He picked up the cloak and walked home, each step heavier than the last.

That night tears fell in their little house. The next day and the day after he and his mother cried but on the third day she said, 'Life must go on. There is nothing to eat. Take your father's hunting tackle and catch some birds to sell.'

'But mum, I've been at school and never learnt to catch birds,' said the boy.

'Do your best,' said his mother.

So the boy set a trap. He put a snare up in a tree. He did something that his father would never have done; he spread a net over the mouth of a large cave high in the mountains. He walked down again but the first trap was empty. He went to the tree and found a little brown Iraq babbler flapping its wings in terror. 'Don't fear, little one, no one will buy you as a pet,' he said and he set it free. As he climbed up to the cave he felt a terrible despair. But there, caught in the net, was a huge bird. What a bird! It was enormous, larger than the boy himself!

'Ahmed,' said the great bird piteously, 'I beg you, set me free. My meat tastes bad, but if you let me go I will fetch a bird that is one hundred times more beautiful than me.'

'How is it that you speak Arabic to me?' asked the boy. 'And how do you know my name?'

'My name is the Bashak,' answered the bird. 'I came here because the wind told me about you and I wished to see you.'

At this Ahmed took out his knife and cut through the net. Then he watched as the Bashak spread his mighty wings and flew off, becoming smaller and smaller and finally disappearing on the horizon.

The next day he returned and sure enough the Bashak had kept his word. There in his claws lay a tiny rainbow-coloured bird with a shining golden beak. The boy took the bird gently in his hands. 'Dear Bashak, how can I ever thank you for this?'

As he walked back down the boy thought, 'Such a bird is too precious to sell. I will give it to the king.'

For the first time in his life he walked to the king's palace. His clothes were ragged, but when the servants saw his glittering bird he was shown into the king's apartments. There Ahmed fell on his knees, offering his gift up to the king. The king was enchanted with the beautiful bird and ordered that a purse filled with gold be given to the boy.

Beside the king sat his powerful wazir, who said, 'Oh king, what a kind boy! Tell him that tomorrow he must bring another bird, just the same but a little smaller. This bird is a male and he must bring the female. Then she will lay eggs and we will have many such beautiful small birds.'

The king turned to his wazir and said in a low voice, 'Don't you see this is a poor boy who has by luck chanced upon this bird? How can he find another one?'

'I will show him,' smiled the wazir and he drew Ahmed into a small chamber and said, 'Our mighty king has decreed that you must bring a female bird of the same kind as this one by tomorrow. If you fail then your head will not be safe on your shoulders.'

Ahmed returned home terribly frightened. His mother tried to comfort him but to no avail. So he set off up hill and down dale into the high mountains and there was the Bashak waiting for him.

'Well, Ahmed, was the king happy?' Ahmed told him what had happened and the great bird said, 'I flew far to find that bird and I am tired, but I will go again. Meet me here tomorrow at noon.' Sure enough, the next day the Bashak brought the same kind of bird but this time a female. Ahmed thanked him from his heart and took it to the king.

Again the king was delighted and the wazir said, 'Ah king, what a splendid youth! Tell him that tomorrow he must bring a cage that is suitable for such wondrous birds.'

But the king stared at his wazir and murmured, 'Don't you see this boy is poor? Where would he find a cage befitting these paragons?'

'I will tell him,' said the wazir and he drew Ahmed into a small chamber and told him that if he didn't manage to find such a cage his head would not be safe on his shoulders. Trembling he returned to his mother but she could not comfort him.

Once again he set off up hill and down dale into the high mountains where the great bird was waiting.

'Was the king still not satisfied?' asked the Bashak and when Ahmed told him how it was the bird sighed and said, 'I have flown now for two whole days and nights and Allah knows I am tired, but my love for you is so great that again I will fly.'

Once more he spread his great wings and the boy watched him fly far off to the horizon. The next day he returned and this time in his beak was a silver cage studded with turquoise and diamonds. Ahmed thanked him from the bottom of his heart and took the cage to the king at once.

Even the king had never beheld such a cage. But the wazir said charmingly, 'Oh king, what a clever youth! I knew he would manage this task. Such birds and such a cage can be owned by no ordinary person. They must surely be owned by the most beautiful princess in this world. Tell the boy to fetch her for us tomorrow.'

The king was aghast. 'Look at that boy!' he said 'Do you not see he has no shoes on his feet? How in the world can he bring us the loveliest damsel there is?'

'Ah, I will let him know, Your Majesty, trust me,' smiled the wazir and he drew Ahmed into a small chamber and threatened him with his life if he did not find her. This time Ahmed returned weeping to his mother and, though she tried to comfort him, he again walked out over hill and down dale until he came to the high mountain where the Bashak was waiting.

'I'm sorry, Ahmed,' said the great bird. 'I cannot fetch her. Tell the king that if he can make a boat of sandalwood with a sail of golden brocade, then we can try to find her.' So Ahmed returned to the palace. The wazir saw him empty-handed and was secretly delighted.

'Your Majesty,' said the youth, 'if I am to fetch this princess I must sail in a ship of sandalwood and golden brocade.'

The king paused a moment and said, 'This is a very costly ship, young man, but you shall have it. My wazir will surely have it built for you, as he is full of ideas.' Beneath his smiles the wazir grew pale but he nodded enthusiastically.

This ship was so expensive that the wazir was forced to sell all his treasures, but when at last it was complete people came from far and wide to gaze on it. Ahmed jumped aboard with the sailors and they hoisted the gleaming golden sails. As they set off the Bashak flew down and perched on the bows as the navigator. The ship cut through the waves like a knife and soon they arrived at the land where the princess lived. She and her people were waiting on the shore, admiring the wondrous vessel.

'Now is your chance,' said the Bashak. 'Invite the princess on board. She will be so overwhelmed! Before she knows it we can sail away with her.' So Ahmed jumped ashore.

However as soon as he saw the princess he could not bring himself to kidnap her. So he told her the truth – that his king had taken her birds and her cage and wished to have her too.

The princess looked at Ahmed and said, 'I will come with you, on one condition. You must fetch me the Water of Life and the Fire of Hell.'

'What?' gasped Ahmed. 'Why that's impossible.'

'For you, no. That is my condition.'

'Ah boy,' said the Bashak, 'this is a hard task! If only you had lured her onto the boat. But, very well, since I love you jump on my back.' So Ahmed climbed onto the mighty bird and the people watched as they flew together up to the highest mountain. There they found the lake whose name is 'The Water of Life'. In Iraq they say that in heaven a gentle rain falls every day. Angels fly down from heaven, land on the earth and shake the rain from their wings. The water drips down and collects in this lake.

'Now, Ahmed, listen carefully,' said the Bashak. 'This girl coming towards you now has pots to collect the Water of Life. You must buy a pot but on no account kiss her.'

Ahmed offered money to buy a pot but the girl demanded a kiss from him. As he grabbed the pot the girl simply disappeared into thin air. He filled it with water, jumped onto the Bashak and they flew down to a deep valley. There in a cleft they saw the burning fires of hell. Ahmed took a stick and went downwards into the dark crevasse. Hotter and hotter it grew and so dark he could see nothing. At last it was so stiflingly hot he could hardly breathe. In the distance he saw a burning fire and reaching into the scorching coals he lit the brand and staggered upwards towards the light.

Ahmed and the Bashak flew back to the princess and she saw that he had found both the Water of Life and the Fire of Hell. Of her own free will she jumped onto the ship and together they sailed to the king.

When they arrived at the palace the king said, 'Fair princess, it is I who have taken your beautiful birds and your cage. What can I give you in return?'

'Oh king, I wish for one of your people as my husband,' said the princess. 'But he must be willing to go through fire for my sake.'

'Well, Ahmed,' asked the king, 'are you willing to go through fire for this lady?'

Ahmed looked at the princess and over at the old Bashak. 'Yes.'

So the king's servants gathered a huge pile of logs and the princess lit them with the fiery brand from hell. Ahmed walked into the flames. At once his flesh was burned from his bones. Then the princess came forward with a little rake. She raked all Ahmed's bones forth from the fire and laid them out with uttermost care on the earth, each one in its place. Then she took the Water of Life and sprinkled it onto the skeleton and at once the flesh was restored to the bones and Ahmed jumped up, even more handsome than before.

At this the king's wazir was filled with fury. He took no pains to hide it and shouted, 'Where is justice, Your Majesty? This wretched boy walks in here and is to marry the loveliest lady on all the earth and I, the most important man in the kingdom, barring you, I am not even considered!'

'Are you willing to go through fire for this princess?' repeated the king.

'Of course I am!' shouted the wazir, and he charged into the flames.

Do you think the princess took out her little rake this time? No, instead she gently dropped the pot containing the Water of Life onto the ground. It cracked into a hundred pieces and the water ran out and became a great lake which is still there in Iraq to this day.

At the wedding Ahmed's mother and the Bashak were the guests of honour. As they tied the marriage knot the princess called out, 'On this day I wish that all creatures may enjoy their happiness and freedom!' And she opened the silver cage and the two rainbow-coloured birds flew higher and higher in the sky, singing love songs for the happy couple.

Bashak Quiz

1. What was Ahmed's father's work?
2. Did his mum and dad go to school when they were young?
3. How many times did the Bashak help Ahmed?
4. How did he get the fire from hell?
5. Did Ahmed trick the princess?
6. Why did the Wazir try to get rid of Ahmed?

Myths from the Land of You

Try and tell this story as if it came from your country. You can change the characters so the father has another job, the Bashak can be another bird, the wazir might be the prime minister and so on.

Home for a Bird Family

Old hollow trees where birds can nest are becoming harder to find. A lot of birds would like to use the holes made by woodpeckers, but many old trees have been cut down so there are fewer holes. If you make a birdhouse you make a place for a bird to lay its eggs and bring up a new family.

1. If you buy a birdhouse go straight to point number 6.
2. If you want to make one get hold of a 12–15cm/4½–6" wide untreated board. Cedar or pine is good wood to use, but you might want to use an old plank; any wood is fine. It should be about 2cm/¾" thick to be warm enough. You can use the same plank for walls, roof and floor.
3. The roof should be sloping and to make it last longer you can paint it. If you have some old roofing felt you can put that on instead. Make sure there are some holes in the bottom of the house so water can get out. Screw it together using galvanised screws so they don't go rusty.
4. Make sure that the roof can be opened, as you need to clean it out after a year or two to make sure there are no diseases.
5. The 'front door' hole can be different sizes depending on what kind of bird you would like to move in. If you make the hole 5cm/2" wide you may get a starling. If it's 3.2cm/1¼" wide you may get a great tit or 2.8cm/1" is big enough for a blue tit.
6. It's a good idea to put up your nesting box well before the birds start laying. Depending on where you live this may be around February.
7. Make sure you fix your birdhouse well so it doesn't damage the tree and is a bit private for the birds. Don't put it next to another branch or a woodpecker may steal the eggs and make sure the local cat can't reach it.
8. If a bird moves in, leave them in peace. If you want to see what's happening get hold of some binoculars but don't disturb the birds, especially the first year, or they may not dare to come back.

If you don't get a family the first year, be patient; they will probably move in next year!

Did you manage to guess the fiendishly hard riddle?

In marble walls as white as milk,

Lined with a skin as soft as silk,

Within a fountain crystal clear,

A golden apple doth appear.

No doors there are to this stronghold,

Yet thieves break in and steal the gold.

The answer is something you may already have eaten today. Perhaps you have broken into it, smashing the top of your breakfast egg, to steal the golden yolk.

Story Earth

You may have felt like a bird during some of these last stories. That is good. But one of the most dangerous traps for a storyteller is that they get too big for their boots and think that they are immensely special and can more or less fly. Now is the time to get down to earth. Without earth, there is nothing for us, the animals or the birds to eat.

To bring you down to earth here are three earth riddles:

1. A dead thing on a living thing on a dead thing on a living thing on a dead thing on a living thing. What are these things?

2. What's the beginning of the earth and the end of the whole globe?

3. What can you see but never reach however long you walk?

If you can't guess them, you can dig up the answers at the end of *Story Earth*.

Ear to the Ground

Do you want to know a secret? The earth was made from a reindeer! Reindeers are incredible. Their bones and antlers are stronger than concrete and far more flexible. The fur of the reindeer is warm, soft and silky, especially the bit under the throat. The Sami people put this in the cradle to keep the baby warm. And they are champion runners – on its very first day, a reindeer calf can outrun an Olympic sprinter!

The Creator of the Sami people, whose name is Ipmil, made the earth from a female reindeer. Her blood poured out into the rushing rivers and seas. Her bones grew into sturdy rocks and mountains. Her flesh became the earth and each hair in her soft fur grew upwards as a tree and then transformed into forests all over the land. Her bright reindeer eyes became the stars. At last Ipmil took her pulsing red heart and buried it at the centre of the earth, warm and steadily beating.

Sami people say that when times are difficult you can still lie with your ear to the ground and listen. If you don't hear the reindeer's heartbeat, you may be in danger. If her heart is beating then all will be well.

The Rat Princess

The 'Rat Princess' is a story you might want to tell to younger children. If they are not used to hearing stories it can be good to start by showing them a real thing. What kind of thing? If you have a pet rat, that would be perfect but there are lots of other possibilities. You could bring a bowl with some old cooked food and say this is the kind of food rats love – the same kind of food we love. Once you have their attention, you can pause a little moment and then start the story. At the end you could ask them if they want to go out and dig in the mud and earth in the garden. They will probably say yes and enjoy getting incredibly dirty.

There once lived a king and a queen who had absolutely *everything*. Massive amounts of everything. However there was only one thing they actually wanted – the thing they couldn't get: a baby.

One morning they were sitting in silence at either end of their immense breakfast table while servants ran in and out with barrels of orange juice and mountains of toast. Then, all at once, a little rat scuttled across the floor. The king jumped up to chase it away but the queen called out, 'No!' Then her majesty sat on the floor and held out a little piece of buttered toast. Slowly, the little rat crept nearer and nearer, until at last it dared to nibble from the queen's hand.

'Look, dear, isn't she adorable?' said the Queen. 'Her coat is shiny. Her eyes are sparkling. Why don't we adopt her as our daughter?'

The little rat girl put her head on one side, peeped up at the king and blinked with her long dark eyelashes and there was nothing the king could say but, 'Yes, of course!'

Nothing was too good for the little Rat Princess. The royal tailor sewed fashionable tiny dresses for her, the royal carpenter built a tiny princess balcony onto the front of the palace and the royal teacher (who had been unemployed so far) began to teach her how to speak Human. She was a fast learner and before long everyone in the kingdom adored the little Rat Princess. Every Thursday she came out onto her little balcony and waved down to the crowds below.

In no time she had grown up and her parents said she should get married.

'Very well, dear Mamma and Pappa!' squeaked the rat princess. 'But you must realise that I wish to marry the mightiest man in the world.'

'Why that's only natural and right my dear,' said the king. 'And who is the mightiest man in the world, would you say?'

The Rat Princess looked up into the blue sky and answered, 'Obviously the sun himself is the mightiest, Pappa.'

'Consider it settled,' said the king. 'The wedding will be held next week.'

Then the Rat Princess put on her new little rat bikini and went out on her tiny balcony so as to get to know her true love better. But soon she came running in again.

'Pappa! The sun is not the mightiest after all! A huge cloud came and covered him entirely. That cloud is so huge and powerful I fell in love at once. It must be the cloud who is the mightiest.'

'In that case, consider yourself engaged to the cloud,' answered the king kindly.

So the Rat Princess put her little wrap around her shoulders, made from bumblebees' fur, and sat out on the veranda so as to be as close as possible to her new fiancé. But it wasn't long before she came running in again.

'Pappa! Something terrible has happened. The cloud bumped into a mountain and he went completely to pieces. It turns out he wasn't nearly as tough as he pretended. It must be the mountain who is the mightiest after all!'

'Dear child, clearly it is the mountain who is your future husband,' answered the king patiently. 'Tomorrow we will order a splendid picnic and parade over to the mountain to greet him properly.'

Sure enough the next morning the royal cook prepared twenty large tempting picnic hampers and the whole court set out to hold the engagement party on the foothills of the great mountain. Tents were erected and tablecloths spread with glasses, champagne and all kinds of good things to eat. The rat princess scampered off to get to know the mountain she was to marry.

After several hours she had still not returned and the king and queen were just becoming worried when she came galloping back calling out, 'Mamma! Pappa! You'll never believe it! The mountain is not the mightiest after all! I climbed up and up and what should I see but enormous numbers of holes and tunnels everywhere. Of course I wondered who be strong enough to eat into the mountain itself, so I crept into one of the tunnels and there who should I meet but the handsomest and strongest rat you can imagine. HE is the mightiest of all!'

'Of course!' called out the king and queen together. 'Why have we not realised this before? Let us meet him at once!'

They did and the royal wedding was held that very day. Not only that, but before the year was over, the king and queen had dozens of tiny grandchildren running all over the palace.

True or False?

1. The king and queen had so many children they had to get twenty-four babysitters.
2. The little rat had twinkly eyes.
3. The Rat Princess thought the sun was weak and ugly.
4. The people hated the Rat Princess and put out rat poison.
5. The king was kind to his daughter.
6. The Rat Princess was quite fussy about boyfriends.
7. She ended up marrying a volcano.

Dirty Earth

Along, long, long, long, long time ago … in fact so long ago that there were no cars or buses. How did people travel? Some rode on a donkey, a horse or a camel. Most people walked. This was such a long time ago that even shoes had not been invented. Everyone was barefoot and that was fine except when a camel trod on their toes. Then they shouted, 'Owwwww!' so loudly that the camel jumped up in the air.

Even the raja (which means 'king') of India had no shoes.

Every morning he woke up and said, 'What a strong handsome and clever raja I am!' Every morning there was a knock on the door and in came a small man. The man's name was Satish Satash and he was the prime minister. Satish Satash bowed low and asked, 'Would Your Majesty like to have a bath?'

'No! I hate washing!' shouted the raja.

Every morning the raja absolutely refused to wash and so, of course he got dirtier and dirtier. He smelt horrible. His beard was like a stinking old carpet. His face was so dirty that if you had taken a seed, planted it on his cheek and watered it, it would have started sprouting.

One day, as usual, the raja woke up and said, 'What a strong, handsome and clever raja I am!' and as usual the door was opened by Satish Satash, who bowed low and asked, 'Would Your Majesty like to have a bath?'

'No! I hate washing!' shouted the raja.

Then the raja went and sat on his throne where all the mighty men and women from the whole rajadom were assembled. On that day the raja noticed that all the mighty men and women had clothes pegs pinned to their noses.

'Satish Satash! Why are they wearing clothes pegs?' whispered the raja.

'Ah!' stumbled Satish Satash. 'What a good question! Well, it's like this – the whole council is fearful that the raja is going to be ill, since he doesn't take a bath.'

'And why have you never said this before? The raja shall bathe, this very day!'

shouted the raja. And all the mighty men and women cheered, 'Hurrah!' and took off the clothes pegs.

Then the great doors of the palace were opened and out marched two drummers and three trumpeters playing a royal washing march. Then came the raja and all the courtiers singing. This was such a long time ago there were no baths or showers so they went down to the river. When the people in the town heard the procession they came running to see what was happening.

As they reached the river bank the raja threw off all his royal robes and jumped into the river with a great splash. He scrubbed and washed himself in the clean water. When he was finished he jumped up onto the land. But as soon as he trod onto the earthy bank his feet became dirty at once.

The raja was furious that the river bank was so dirty and shouted, 'The raja is sparkling clean, but the land is dirty! It does not befit a raja who is so strong, handsome, clever and clean to live in a dirty country. It is unworthy and yukky. Satish Satash, you have three days to wash the country and if you don't do it, you will lose your head!'

'Of course, Your Majesty,' said Satish Satash sadly.

Poor little Satish Satash, how could he wash the whole country? But luckily everyone felt sorry for him and promised to help. They fetched their brushes and their brooms and set to brushing every corner of the whole country. In fact they brushed so energetically that they whirled up a huge cloud of dust.

When the evening came the raja was so angry that he shouted, 'Satish Satash! I ordered that you should clean the whole country, not fill the whole sky with dust! You have two days to finish the job and if you don't do it then you will lose your head.'

'Naturally, Your Majesty,' said Satish Satash miserably.

Poor little Satish Satash, how could he wash the whole country in just two days? But everyone felt sorry for him so they fetched their buckets and their scrubbing brushes and set to work. They washed so thoroughly that there was water everywhere. And when you mix water and earth what do you get? Mud!

When evening came and the palace gates opened and the raja came out to see how the cleaning was going – squish! Squish, squish, squish went the mud between the royal toes. The raja was fumingly furious!

'I ordered that you should wash the land, not cover it with mud! You have one more day to utterly clean the land and if you don't do it then – chop off his head!'

'How just, Your Majesty,' said Satish Satash dismally.

Poor little Satish Satash, how on earth could he wash the whole country in just one day? But then he suddenly remembered his old aunty who used to put an old sheepskin over her dirty floor. So he asked everyone to fetch all their old sheepskins and leather and sewing needles and they stitched and sewed the whole night and the next day too until leather covered the land.

Evening came, the palace gates opened and the raja stepped outside. The raja walked here, and the raja walked there, back and forth and wherever he walked his feet were clean.

'Satish Satash, you are a genius, I always knew it!' Then the raja called for a gold medal for noble service but just as the drummers were rolling their drums, the trumpeters were blowing their trumpets and the raja was bending over to pin a great medal onto Satish Satash's chest, there came a cry, 'STOP!'

From behind the crowd came a wrinkled old lady. 'Now you listen to me!' she said to the raja. 'You think Satish Satash is a genius but you are wrong. Satish Satash is silly and so are you! Today I was hungry so I went out into my garden to dig up a carrot. But how could I? My whole garden was covered in sheepskin and leather! Dilly, my holy cow, was terribly hungry but all her clover and grass was covered so she had nothing to eat. Is everyone going to starve so the raja can have clean feet? Now you stand quite still!'

The raja stood stiff as a rod from fear. No one had ever dared to speak to him like this before. The old lady took a sharp knife from her pocket and cut a shape in the leather around his feet. Then she took a leather lace and bound the leather onto his feet. She rolled back the rest of the leather and the raja began to walk both here and there without getting dirty feet. In this way the very first shoes were made.

Everyone agreed that the raja had been very silly, so he had to move out of the palace and they asked the old lady to be rani (queen) instead. And she taught everyone that Earth is not dirty. In fact it's perfectly fantastic to grow food and beautiful flowers.

Rats don't wear shoes. In fact no animals, birds or insects wear shoes. Why?

Maybe the invention of shoes was not such a great thing. Some scientists say that walking barefoot makes any extra electricity in our body go down into the earth and we get healthier. Maybe that's why we are so happy running around on the beach barefoot. I love walking barefoot and I once made my kids take off their shoes and walk in the snowy Norwegian forest. Then I tried it myself and I had to scream! It was so painful!

Still some storytellers like to take off their shoes when telling a story. Now for a real scientific story ...

The Story of Earth

Millions of years ago the air had so much carbon dioxide in it, and so little oxygen, that no kinds of animals could breathe. At that time there lived a tiny little creature about the size of a human blood corpuscle. This little creature had a hard shell made of calcium and a tiny body made partly of carbon.

Countless trillions of these little shell creatures lived in the water and when they died they fell to the bottom of the ocean. So many of them fell to the bottom that gradually they built up a thick layer on the ocean floor. In this way, that tiny bit of carbon in their body which they had taken out of the water was stored safely at the bottom of the ocean. As more and more of these tiny creatures lived and then died, so more and more carbon was taken out of the water and stored at the bottom of the ocean, and so more and more carbon was sucked out of the air and into the water to replace it. These little creatures in the sea were also constantly breathing out oxygen into the water, and this oxygen bubbled up from the water into the air. After millions of years, the air had changed so much that dinosaurs, birds and animals were able at last to live and breathe.

Meanwhile, the remains of the sea creatures at the bottom of the ocean hardened together to make a kind of rock called limestone. At the same time, powerful forces deep inside the earth were pushing the ocean floor and so large amounts of the limestone were pushed up onto the land. These little sea creatures had made a new kind of earth from their tiny shells. They had also made the ocean and the air different, so many new forms of life came into being.

One life form that came very recently we call people. After thousands of years of living on the planet these people found all sorts of ways to change the earth. They used minerals and metals, and also the limestone rock made from the little shells. They cut the limestone into rough blocks and made beautiful shapes to live in. Most places in the world still have houses made of these materials.

Then people found that if they heated the limestone they could make glue, glue with amazing powers, glue that could mix with other materials to make very hard rock. They called this glue cement. When cement was being made, the limestone was heated so hot that all of the carbon from the shells, which had been safely stored for so many millions of years, was released once more into the air. The cement is such powerful glue that people have been able to build higher and higher, so far up to 163-storey buildings.

When you make one ton of cement, it releases nearly a ton of carbon dioxide into the air, the very thing that the shell creatures had so carefully stored away. So people had started turning their world back into a place where it's hard for people and animals to live ...

Luckily, some people realised we don't need to use cement to build; we can do what people have done all over the world – build beautiful houses out of earth without cement. Making earth houses doesn't release any carbon dioxide. Not only that, they keep out the radiation of mobile phones, so they are very comfortable and safe to live in.

Myths from the Land of You

This last story I heard from my brother. He has been building earth houses all his adult life. He is getting quite famous and they have made him into a professor for his work. OK, he is my brother but I think he is fantastic. Maybe you know someone who is doing something you think is really cool and you can make it into a story and tell people about it.

My Land

Two men walked with long strides towards each other from opposite sides of a field. One was carrying a spade, the other a hoe. They met in the middle, anger flashing in their eyes.

'This is my land!' said the first. 'Move aside!'

'Not at all!' said the other. 'This is my land, given to me by my father; it is you who should move aside.'

'Given to you by your father?' said the first. 'That well-known thief, who stole the land from my grandfather?'

'But your grandfather tricked my poor old great-grandfather into giving it away when he was old and frail,' said the second man.

'Listen here!' said the first. 'This land belonged to my ancestors. It is written in the stories.'

'Your stories, perhaps,' snapped the other.

The two argued into the night, neither budging a foot from the piece of ground he stood on.

In the morning they were still quarrelling and their voices could be heard ringing out across the fields the whole day. Neither man dared move in case the other took his place. Their wives came with food, but they ate little.

A girl walked by. She stopped for a while and listened to them arguing on and on. Then she said quietly, 'Perhaps you should seek help. Old Hodja lives in the wood across the path.'

The two men walked down a small path through the cool shady forest until they reached a clearing. Hodja sat outside his hut, twisting rope with his fingers. He looked up. The two men stumbled forward, shouting, 'It's my land.'

Hodja nodded. 'Take me there,' he said. When they reached the field, Hodja pointed to a bare patch in the middle, where the land was dry and compressed from their stamping feet. 'Here?' he said and they both nodded.

Hodja flung himself down suddenly, lying with his ear to the ground.

He was there a long time until one of the men asked what he was doing.

'I'm listening to what the earth has to say,' said Hodja and he put his ear back on the ground.

Eventually he stood up.

'Well ... and ... what does the earth say?' stammered the men.

'The earth says ...' said Hodja, 'she does not belong to either of you. You belong to her.'

An apprentice is someone who works with a master or a mistress to learn how to do something. By now you may have become an apprentice Natural Storyteller. It will really help you to learn if you find a good storyteller to listen to. Just sit and listen as much as you can. You will learn a lot. They may tell huge long stories like this next one, but it's best that you don't try and tell these mega epic long ones before you have tried a few shorties.

Roots Make Flowers

In India lived a woman who had no husband, no patch of earth to call her own, no cow, not even a pair of gold earrings. To make a living, she took clay from the ground and made simple pots which she sold in the market. That woman had a blessing – two daughters.

One day the younger girl said, 'Sister, look at our darling mother. She works so hard and is growing old so fast! Last night I dreamt that the Earth Goddess, you know, BhuDevi, rose out of the ground. I knew it was her, sister, and she told me how to help mother. Come!'

She led her sister out into the sun and explained: 'The Earth Goddess said I should sit on the bare earth and listen to the voice of the earth. She said that you must take mother's big round pot and go to the rushing river. Fill the pot right up to the brim but don't touch the water even with your fingernails. Then pour the water over me! Let's see what happens!'

She sat on the bare earth, closed her big dark eyes and listened to the voice of the earth.

Her sister took the large pot, went down to the rushing Ganges river and filled it carefully so that not even her fingernails touched the water. She carried it up and as the younger sister opened her dark eyes she poured water over her head. In that moment the girl transformed into a flowering tree!

Her sister picked dazzling bright flowers from the tree and laid them gently in the shade. Then she fetched more water and threw it onto the tree, and at once her sister reappeared, laughing and shaking drops of water from her hair. Then the two girls sat and threaded a garland with the sweet scented flowers.

In the nearby town a rich Brahmin boy was bored. Through the latticed window came a breeze and on it a smell so sweet and unknown that the boy hurried down into the courtyard. Soon he was towering over those two poor girls selling their garland of flowers. 'Where do these flowers come from?' he demanded. The girls didn't answer. The young Brahmin was used to people doing what he said and he became angry. He snatched the flowers, threw down some money and went inside. He took up a tattered shawl, and as the girls left, he followed them on the dusty road home. He had never seen such a poor hut before, but all day and then all night he hid outside.

With the dawn he saw their mother scurry out like a little brown mouse. Soon the two girls emerged. The younger sat on the bare earth and the older threw water cascading over her younger sister from top to toe.

There before his very eyes, he saw the girl transform! Her feet turned into twisting roots delving down into the red earth, her soft, golden skin turned to hard shining bark and her two legs merged into one. From the shiny tree trunk pushed forth branches and twigs. Then the twig buds burst and unfolded into glossy green leaves, and beside them fresh buds exploded into dazzling red flowers.

Some days passed and late in the evening the poor mother sat wearily eating her bowl of rice. In the street was a loud clattering and commotion. Then a thundering knock on her door and it burst open. Two men entered, grasped the old woman and marched her to the town. In the high dome of the house, unwashed, she stood before the rich Brahmin himself.

'My son is a stubborn boy,' said the rich man. 'He insists that you and your family come and live here in our palace. Well, to be honest, it's more than that; he wishes to marry your daughter.'

Back home the mother called out, 'You wicked girls, what have you been doing while I am out? Isn't my life hard enough as it is, without you making trouble? Don't you see, they are rich Brahmins? This can never work!' But the next morning she said, 'From our lowly caste you are chosen.'

So they moved to the Brahmins' house and their life changed. Even though the girl was born in a poor hut the gorgeous bridal sari of the Brahmins suited her perfectly and the wedding lasted for three days. What a wedding! Dancers, musicians, cooks, all dressed in bright clothes. There was fasting, there was feasting, a raga for good luck was sung, wedding drums were beaten and rice with turmeric was thrown onto the bride and groom.

Among the many guests was the rich boy's sister. This sister was a rani, a local queen, married to a raja in the next town. This rani had everything money could buy. She was dressed in a glittering sari and she whispered to other wedding guests, 'How is this possible, this miserable girl marrying my brother? Do you know the poor caste she is from?'

At night the bride and groom were alone in a darkened room. They lay quite still on the bridal bed and did not say a word. The second night was the same. For three nights they stayed in their room without speaking.

At last the poor girl broke the wall of silence. 'Why? Why did you marry me if you won't even speak to me?'

'Why did you marry me?' answered the boy. 'You say nothing but I know you can transform yourself into a flowering tree?'

She smiled and told him her secret, asking him to follow the instructions carefully. She sat on the ground and listened to the voice of the earth. He went and fetched water and there in the room she transformed into a tree. With the tips of his fingers he carefully picked each flower and threw the water over her until she appeared, laughing and shaking the drops of water from her hair. Then they lay on the bed of flowers. Next morning his sister the rani watched showers of petals falling from their bedroom window.

'Dear sister,' she said, 'just for you I am preparing a picnic in the jungle. All my rich girlfriends will be here. I will give you a pretty sari to wear and we will put henna on your hands. Come!' Picnic hampers were packed and in the jungle servants climbed like monkeys to hang swings from the branches of the trees. The rich girls jumped onto the swings screaming. Long shadows fell, fires were lit for chai and the rich sister announced in a loud voice, 'And now, my new sister-in-law will turn herself into a flowering tree!'

'What?' said the girl. 'No human can change themselves into a tree.'

'I have seen you do it for my brother. Do it now!'

'Very well. For you, the sister of my beloved. But I beg you, please take care as you pick my flowers; do not break or damage the twigs and leaves.'

So beside the fire the girl turned into a flowering tree. The rich girls were amazed. They screamed louder. They rushed at the pretty tree, snapping twigs, twisting leaves, ripping branches and cracking the very roots of the tree. Just then the heavy monsoon rain began to pour down and the girls scattered, running towards the palace.

Impatiently the Brahmin's son waited for his bride to come back from the picnic.

'Don't ask me, brother,' said his sister. 'We came home separately after the monsoon rain broke. She must have got lost.'

Outside the rain was pouring from the sky. As it fell onto the bark of the fallen tree the bark transformed into skin and the tree trunk became a legless broken body with only stumps for arms. The monsoon flood washed the poor girl's broken body into a gulley and she floated downstream.

At the road a group of taxi drivers were huddled against the weather. One of them saw her and pulled her from the water. He ran through the puddles to fetch a shawl and carried her splashing to his cycle rickshaw. His fellow drivers laughed and made fun of him. But shrugging he cycled off to the nearest town. There, leaving her on the steps of the palace of the rani, he said, 'Here you will surely be cared for. May BhuDevi the Earth Goddess bless you.'

Next morning the maid came out to sweep the steps and saw the poor girl lying there. She ran in for balm and bound healing leaves onto the younger sister's wounds. As she brought the morning tea for the rani she asked if she could bring the girl inside.

'What?' said the rani. 'Someone without arms and legs is not a proper human! I don't want her in here ...'

Meanwhile the rich Brahmin boy went into the jungle. Calling the name of his lost bride he roamed far and wide, saying, 'BhuDevi, Earth Goddess, help me! Where is my love, the Flowering Tree?' But no one helped him.

So he walked on. No longer a rich boy, he rarely ate or drank, and his shining blue-black skin turned grey. His hair and beard became matted, his clothes ragged, his eyes wild and at last he stopped speaking altogether.

Years passed. She sitting on the steps, he walking. BhuDevi the Earth Goddess looked down on them and at last she could bear it no longer. The goddess turned the steps of the lost bridegroom towards the palace of his sister. The maid stood watching on the porch. 'Mistress, there is a wild sadhu, a holy man, passing. He looks like your lost brother.'

He was brought in, washed and rubbed with sandalwood oil until his skin shone blue black and his sister the rani was sure it was her brother. Her servants prepared the finest food and drink but he said nothing. Earth trodden underfoot makes more sound than he did. A pebble washed downstream and clinking onto its fellows speaks louder than he did. A sickle cutting the grass makes more sound.

That night the softest rugs were laid out for him to rest on. His sister's prettiest maid was sent in to sing to him but he sat and stared ahead saying nothing.

Then her maid asked, 'Mistress, may I bring in the creature who sits on the steps? She has such a beautiful voice; perhaps she can make him speak?'

So the girl with no arms or legs was placed beside him but still he said nothing. He stared at her as if he was blind.

Suddenly she speaks. With the sound of her voice it's as if he is starting from sleep. He stares at her, tears streaming down his face. His spell is broken. He lifts her gently outside. In the courtyard he finds a full-bellied jar. Down at the river he fills it, taking care that his fingernails don't touch the water. As she opens her dark eyes they're met by his. He pours the water over her body. She is transformed into a tree. A tree that is bent, its branches cracked, its roots broken. He binds the broken branches and twigs with locks of his hair. Each day through the dry season, he fetches water and lovingly tends the tree. The bark begins to heal its wounds; the branches grow, mend and become firm. New leaves and flowers burst from their buds.

The earth turns; it is the monsoon season again. The storm breaks. He stands watching as the rain washes down onto the tree. He watches as the blossom and twigs shrink back into the trunk. He watches as the roots shrink back and become feet. Over the whole tree, the hard, shiny bark softens into golden skin. The trunk divides into two legs and two branches become arms. At the crown of the tree appears her lovely head laughing and shaking the drops of water from her hair.

Do you think their love was greater and deeper after that long separation? Of course it was.

And what about the sisters, the old mother, the maid, what happened to all of them? In the Indian villages they say, 'Ask the Earth Goddess BhuDevi. She takes care of everyone who takes care of the earth.'

This is a very long story! A Story Skeleton will help us remember it.

Think of seven things or characters in the story, then seven actions, then seven feelings. Write them in the same order they come in the story. You can do one first and then see if we remember the same things. It's such a long story I have definitely left some things out.

Story Skeleton

7 nouns (things or characters)	**7 verbs** (actions)	**7 feelings**
Poor woman	Making pots	Love
Two sisters	Dreaming	Courage
The Earth Goddess	Listening to the earth	Fascination
Flowering tree	Selling flower garland	Jealousy
Rich boy	Waiting	Patience
Rani (queen)	Tricking	Care
Maid	Gardening	Love

Earth Story-Making

Some people, like the rani in this story or the king in the 'Dirty Earth' story, think they are better than others. They think that earth is dirty. 'How disgustingly muddy and revolting!' they say.

That's a bit crazy when you think that earth gives us all our food. All our food grows from earth, including meat, since animals eat stuff that's grown on the earth too. Not only that, earth also grows the trees that give us air to breathe, beauteous flowers and is one of the best and cleanest building materials you can find. This part of *The Natural Storyteller* book is celebrating earth.

If you want to join in, you can make an earth story. Here is one way to do it. Try to do some part of the story-making outside:

1. Find a tray and fill it with earth. Earth can be many different types, sandy, clay, rich with worms, bugs and amazing invisible microbes. Find a few different kinds of earth.
2. Fill a container with water. Start adding the water to the earth, making a landscape. Tiny rivers, muddy marshes, hills or whatever you want. Don't try and make a perfect landscape. Just enjoy making stuff with earth.
3. Wash your hands and find a place to sit and think of an earth story. This could be many different kind of stories. There is no 'right' story – only one you like! Perhaps it's a story that you already know but you focus on the earth in the tale. Perhaps it's a story from this book which you change into your own version. Perhaps it's something that happened to you or someone you know which connects with earth. Perhaps it's something that just pops up in your imagination.
4. Now go back to your tray landscape and see how you can make it into the landscape of this story. Use twigs, seeds, leaves, feathers, bits of old plastic or

whatever is lying around. When you have made something like the landscape in your story, imagine the people or animals. Now imagine all the things that happen in the story. If you want to make a twig or a stone into a character you can play it out in the landscape. Do this without telling the story and make sure you are in a place where you are relaxed and don't feel stupid mucking about with mud!

5. When you've finished, take a break, have a drink from something that's grown on the earth (e.g. tea or juice) and eat a snack that's grown on the earth (e.g. biscuits, fruit, a sandwich).

6. Now, for the first time, tell your story by yourself. You might want to do this walking around or sitting still. This may be the hardest bit because you are not even sure what it is yet.

7. If you are the kind of person who likes writing, write down a few short notes about your story.

8. If you are the kind of person who likes recording, use a mobile phone or other recorder and tell the story into that. Then listen to it and tell it again.

9. Now, grab someone as a guinea pig and tell it to them. Get a bit of feedback.

10. You have now made an earth story! If you like it I hope you will find places to tell it. Most children smaller than you love to hear stories, or maybe you want to write it down. Please send me an email to geo.k@online.no or post it on my Facebook page 'Georgiana Keable The Story of Nature and the Nature of Story', or maybe I will bump into you one day – because I would LOVE to hear it.

Do you remember the riddles of *Story Earth*?

1. A dead thing on a living thing on a dead thing on a living thing on a dead thing on a living thing. What are these things?

2. What's the beginning of the earth and the end of the whole globe?

3. What can you see but never reach however long you walk?

The answers are:
1. A hat on a person on a saddle on a horse on some tarmac on the living earth.
2. The letter E.
3. The horizon.

Story Water

Dear reader, only three more sections and you will have completed the entire apprenticeship for being a *Natural Storyteller*.

There is no way this can happen unless you plunge into the sea or at least a lake. Most of the natural world is covered in water and there are still many strange creatures hiding in the depths of the oceans which no one has yet seen.

Here follow stories about this gorgeous element and those who swim there.

Riddle 1:

What always runs but never walks,

Often murmurs, never talks,

Has a bed but never sleeps,

Has a mouth but never eats?

Riddle 2:

As I was going o'er London Bridge,

I heard something crack;

Not a man in all England

Can mend that.

Riddle 3:

What lives without breath,

Is cold as death?

Moving around,

It wears chain mail without a sound?

Hard riddles, but perhaps soft water will help to wear them down.

Salmon Boy

In autumn the leaves go bright orange, yellow and red. Humans are busily hurrying hither and thither and often don't hear the coming of winter. But far out in the ocean the salmon people hear the autumn calling and swim home.

A boy sits by a fire and his grandmother cuts him a sizzling piece of roasted salmon tail. The juice runs down his fingers and the boy hungrily munches the tasty fish.

'Remember?' says Grandmother.

Of course he remembers. Does she think he is stupid?

'Remember to put the fish-bones back in the river,' she says.

The boy nods but he is thinking, 'What a ridiculous, old-fashioned, superstitious waste of time!' He checks no one is looking, throws the bones behind a bush and runs off to play.

The next day the boy is running again. He runs over the rocks and falls head first into the sea. He is plunging down, a strong boy, but the sea is stronger. Foundering and struggling, he is drawn ever further and deeper out to sea by the waves. There is no more air left in his body, he is bursting, he can't breathe! Suddenly he feels a strange nibbling touch all over his skin. He opens his eyes in the salt water and sees he is surrounded by fish. They are gently nudging all over his body.

Tickling fish mouths nibble at his neck and suddenly he feels an opening of gills and he gasps salt water into his body. He can breathe the sea! He feels his warm blood turning cold. His arms are shrinking inwards, turning into fins. His two legs are melding together into a fish's tail. Along his back the dorsal fin breaks through. His mouth is stretching forward and over his skin small shining silver scales are forming. He flips his tail and swims downwards with all the other fishes.

There on the seabed ahead of him he sees what Grandfather has always told him. The salmon people have their own village under the sea, a beautiful village filled with delicious food. He plays with the salmon children. It's so fun darting around the brilliant corals and learning all the fishy games.

One day as he is playing he sees a girl fish who doesn't join the others. Day after day she simply lies on the seabed and watches them. He asks an older fish, who says, 'That girl is lame. She has no bones.' Salmon boy shuts his fish eyes under the water and remembers another life. He knows where her bones are. He threw them behind a bush.

The fish swim north, up to the Arctic. They have adventures with whales and dolphins and grow strong and happy with the good food. Three whole years Salmon Boy stays there. Then suddenly one day he knows it's time to go home. It seems like all the other salmon know the same thing and, without a word, they swim back across the ocean towards the river where they were born.

That autumn the village saw a boy coming up the hill. He walked towards the fire where they sat roasting fish. He was taller and older than the boy they had lost but he seemed so familiar. He stopped and said, 'Yes, it's me, Salmon Boy. For three whole years I swam with the salmon people. I did them wrong but still they fed me generously and showed me respect. The salmon people have great wisdom. We must honour them as they honour us.'

The elders of the village were so happy to see the knowledge of nature had passed to a new generation. Everyone welcomed Salmon Boy back into their village.

The First Nations people told this story for a reason. They told it at the time of the salmon fishing. First they put their nets in the river. The nets always had holes in so that many salmon would get through and could go up the river and make their babies. In order to give the fish plenty of time to get through the net, they would sit down, make a fire and share stories like this one.

Now, almost all the salmon you buy in the shop are not wild salmon. They are fish that are stuck in a 'farm', millions of them. They are fed food they wouldn't naturally eat and get many diseases and are fed lots of medicine. Many of them are deformed and many are blind. 'Salmon Boy' story reminds us of the incredible story of natural salmon and to honour the wild salmon who are still alive.

Myths from the Land of You

If you could transform into a sea animal or fish, which would it be? Imagine that, like Salmon Boy, you fall into a river, a lake or the sea and you meet others of that kind and are transformed suddenly into that sea animal or fish. For three years you live with them, and then you return to your own family and school and tell everyone what happened.

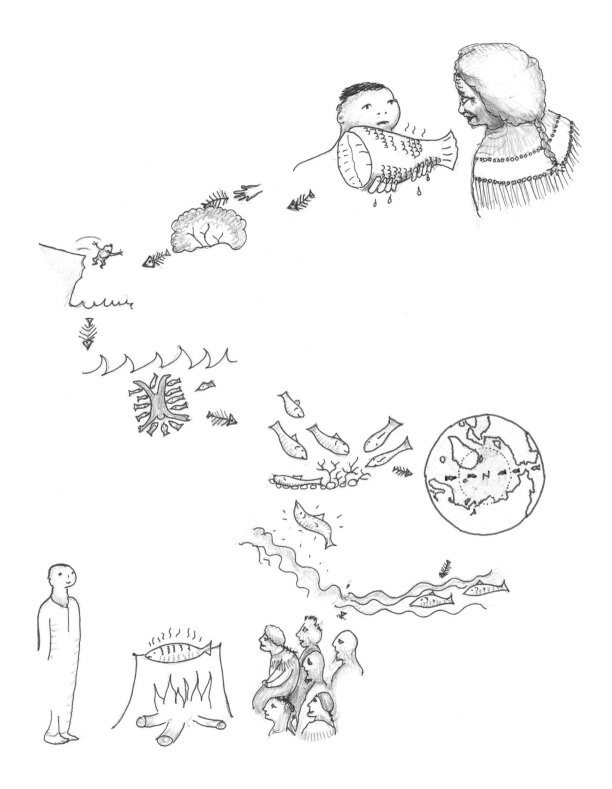

The Flood

Agood man sat in his house alone. Suddenly the door burst open and his children came running in ...

'Daddy,' they said, 'The flood's coming!'

The man said, 'Don't worry, my children. Have faith in God. God will save us.'

His children tried to persuade him to leave but he wanted to stay, so they ran off. Soon, the water was seeping in under the door so, rather than get wet feet, the man went upstairs to pray:

'Oh I believe in you, God, yes I do! Yes I do! You have made technology. You will save me. This is true.'

The water was rising so fast that suddenly the upstairs window burst open and a big, fat, red-faced man put his head in.

'Jo!' he said. 'It's me, Andy! Come on! I've got you a lifeboat! The flood's risin'. Get your skates on. Scarper!'

But the man said calmly, 'That's very kind, Andy, but don't worry about me. I believe in God. He will save me.' So Andy drove away in the lifeboat.

The water started bubbling up through the floorboards. So the man slithered out of the window and started to crawl up the roof. He was really praying in earnest now. 'Oh, great God, I believe in you. Save me!'

Just then he heard a very loud noise. He looked up and saw a helicopter with a rope dangling down and a man with a loud hailer calling, 'Come up here, quickly! We are the emergency police. We are going to save you.'

'No!' shouted the man. 'You don't need to save me. God will save me.' So they went away.

The man prayed. The water rose. Over the treetops, over the tops of the houses. The water entered his nose, his lungs. The man drowned.

When he got up to God in heaven he was really annoyed.

'God,' he said, 'I believed in you. Why didn't you save me?'

And God said, 'My son, I sent your children, I sent your best friend, I sent the emergency police. What more could I do?'

In the old days before schools were invented, people told stories to teach and to discuss things. A good story is one of the most fun ways of learning. But they can also be a dangerous weapon. Bullies like Hitler often use stories to convince people that their horrible plans are a great idea. A story is a powerful thing so take care ...

My dad told me that story. Often if you ask dads and mums if they know any stories they say, ' No, I don't know any.' But really they do know stories; they are just hidden in another part of their brain. Sometimes if you tell them a story it will remind them of one they have forgotten. This next story I got from my mum.

King Fish in the Sea

Off the coast of Norway huge oil fields lie under the sea. Oil is called the 'black gold' and lots of very rich people live in the oil town. But outside the oil town there once lived a fisherman and his wife who were very poor. They lived in a little shed with so many cracks that the wind blew in all winter long. They had never understood how to get unemployment benefit money so they lived from the few fish the man managed to catch.

One day, as usual, he sat with his fishing rod beside the sea. It was a clear spring day and the sea was blue and sheer like a mirror. He waited and waited but nothing happened. Not even a tiny tiddler. He ate his dried fish sandwich and enjoyed himself relaxing in the sun.

Suddenly he got a bite on the rod. He hauled it in and it felt like a big, heavy fish. Pulling it up, silver, blue and pink, he took the hook from its mouth and suddenly it winked at him and said, 'Dear fisherman, I am no ordinary fish. I am King of the Fishes. Please let me go.'

'A fish that can speak I will certainly not eat,' said the fisherman and he took the hook gently from its mouth and watched as it swam down through the water, leaving a thin red trail of blood behind before disappearing into the deep.

When he got back to the hut that night empty-handed, his wife was disappointed. 'Didn't you catch anything at all?' she asked.

'Oh yes, indeed I did,' he replied. 'It was none other than the King of the Fishes so of course I let it go again.'

'What?' said his wife. 'I can't believe it! You caught the King of the Fishes and let him go free without asking him for a single wish?'

'What should I have wished for?'

'We live in a poor, freezing hovel. You should ask him for a little cottage to live in!'

So the fisherman went back down to the ocean. The water was no longer still and clear but was green and yellow. He called out:

King Fish in the sea
Please listen to me
For my wife won't let things be
As I'd like them to be.

In no time at all the fish had swum up to the surface. 'How can I help you, kind fisherman?'

'My wife says that we live in a miserable hovel and would you be so good as to give us a little cottage to live in?'

'Go back. She is in the cottage already,' said the fish.

The fisherman returned and instead of the miserable hut was a little cottage with pink, sweet-smelling roses growing up around the door. His wife stood beaming on the doorstep. She drew him by the arm inside. Inside was a cosy little parlour with a warm fire crackling on the hearth. In the kitchen there were shining pots hanging on the wall and out in the back garden were cherry trees and apple trees and ducks swimming on a little pond.

'Ah, here we will be happy, wife!' said the man.

'You could be right,' said his wife.

Far over the world in Asia lived another fishing family. They had many children but each day they had just enough food. Most days they sang together and lived well.

Back in Norway, weeks passed and one day the fisherman was sitting enjoying himself watching the ducks peck about in the garden when his wife shouted out of the window, 'Husband! This cottage is fine but it's so small! I have invited my relations from Australia. We have no spare room and we will need a car to drive them around and a garage to put it in. Go down to the sea and ask the fish for a bigger house.'

Well, the fisherman didn't really see the point but he didn't like to argue, so off he went.

That day the sea was no longer green and yellow, it was purple and thick. There was seaweed floating on the surface and the seagulls were screeching. He went down to the shore and called out:

King Fish in the sea
Please listen to me
For my wife won't let things be
As I'd like them to be.

In no time the fish had swum up to the surface and said, 'How can I help you, fisherman?'

'My wife says that the little cottage is nice but a bit small. Would it be possible to get a slightly larger house to live in, ideally with a garage?'

'Go back, she is there already,' said the fish.

Where the cottage had stood was a wide drive with a huge security camera glaring down at him. At the end of the drive stood a massive mansion with a mega-long black car that sparkled in the sun. An oil-fired robot flung open the front door and the fisherman entered the large house. There he saw a massive screen with a picture of his wife waving and saying, 'Welcome home, darling.'

A huge silver stove the size of the cottage filled the room. Oil pumped into one side and on the other side popped out a grilled chicken and an oiled-fired robot caught it and said, 'May I offer you a morsel?' Before the man had a chance to answer, the robot said, 'Ah well, never mind, sir,' and threw the chicken into a massive rubbish bin. Then out popped a leg of lamb. 'May I offer you a morsel, sir?' said the robot. And before he could answer, again it was thrown into the massive rubbish bin. But he didn't see his wife.

Robots threw open the veranda doors and there behind the mansion was a huge park where deer and wild horses frisked and ran. Next door was their own personal shopping centre and in the centre a huge swimming pool, shaped like a heart. There in the middle of the pool, lying on a floating bed, was his wife, wearing a bright orange bikini. Swimming towards her over the pool was a waiter, holding above his head a tray and on the tray a glass of gin and tonic.

'Ah wife, now we are in paradise we will be happy,' said the fisherman.

She didn't answer.

In this house they were using so much oil that carbon dioxide was pouring out into the sky and the layer of gases over the world became thicker. This made it harder for the heat to get out, so the world got a little hotter. Some places like the Arctic and the village in Asia where the little fishing family lived got a whole lot warmer. That day the fishing family were so hot in their little boat they came home early.

Clocks ticked, time passed and the fisherman and his wife sat eating breakfast. The table was so long they had to use a microphone to speak to each other.

'Husband, this house is fine,' broadcast the fisherman's wife. 'But we have no power at all here. Go to the fish and tell him we want to be king.'

'Wife! The fish can't do that. Norway has a king already.'

'Look, maybe you don't want to be king, husband, but let me tell you, I do. Go to the fish at once.'

Well the fisherman didn't really want to go but it was so uncomfortable to disagree, so off he went.

Down at the sea the waves were high and a foul stench was blowing onto the shore and the fisherman called out:

King Fish in the sea
Please listen to me
For my wife won't let things be
As I'd like them to be.

In no time the fish had swum up to the surface and said, 'What does she want now, fisherman?'

'Well, she says that the house is great but she has no real political power. Would it be at all possible to make her king?'

'Go back. She is king already,' said the fish.

When the fisherman got back he saw to his amazement that the royal palace had been uprooted from Oslo and stood in place of the mansion. At the back door he saw King Harald and Queen Sonia sadly pulling large suitcases away from their home. Into the side of the palace a massive oil pipe was pumping oil from the sea and on the roof a huge helicopter was landing and unloading tropical plants and fruit from Africa.

As the fisherman entered he met a wall of heat pouring from a massive oil heater. He threw off his waterproofs and wellington boots and walked through to the throne room where his wife sat with a golden crown, surrounded by photographers and journalists. They called out, 'Your Majesty, now you have become king what is your advice for the people?'

'Yes indeed,' she said. 'My people, you must all go shopping every day and use even more petrol. Then you will be much happier, just like me.' And she smiled a cheesy smile into the cameras.

The more gases that flew up from the palace into the sky, the hotter it got down in Asia. The next day it was so hot that there was no rain at all and the seeds that the girls had planted didn't sprout. So the father in the house went to his neighbour to borrow food.

Back at the palace the fisherman made his way through the crowd and said quietly, 'Ah wife, now you are king, now at last you are happy.'

'Do you understand nothing?' shouted his wife. 'Of course I'm not happy. Norway is such a small country there is no real power here at all. Go at once to the fish and say that I must become the president of either America or China, whichever is the most powerful. No arguments, I am the king, go this minute!'

The fisherman felt quite faint. He shivered and shook, his knees and legs trembling. A high wind blew over the land and the clouds flew past overhead. It grew dark, the leaves fell from the trees and the water rose and roared as if it were boiling and splashed upon the shore. In the distance he saw ships that were firing flares in their sore need, pitching and tossing on the waves. And yet in the midst of the sky there was still a small patch of blue, though on every side it was as red as in a heavy storm. Full of despair he went and said:

King Fish in the sea
Please listen to me
For my wife won't let things be
As I'd like them to be.

The fish was there at once saying, 'What does she want now?'

'I know it sounds ridiculous,' said the fisherman. 'But she wondered if you could make her president of the USA or China, whichever is the most powerful.'

'Go back,' said the fish. 'She is president already.'

It was very hard for the fisherman to recognise his home now. The entire Zhongnanhai government complex from China built on three large islands had been moved there. In front were tanks patrolling up and down and soldiers with guns guarding the bridge. They demanded his passport and it took hours and three translators before he could persuade them that he was married to the new president, the most powerful person in the whole world. As they marched him over the bridge he looked up and saw a big cloud of smog hovering over the monolithic buildings and blocking out the sun.

Meanwhile the little family in Asia were so hot they didn't know what to do. They didn't dare to go to the neighbours again to borrow food.

After being thoroughly searched, x-rayed and interviewed, at last the fisherman was allowed into the high-security room and saw his wife covered in military medals with the world press taking her photo.

'Hallo, wife,' he said. 'Now you must be happy there is nothing left for you to be.' But she stood still as a statue and didn't move or say a word.

Early next morning in the presidential bedroom the fisherman was sleeping deeply. He had been running back and forth so much he was sleeping like a log but suddenly his wife dug him in the ribs with her elbow and said, 'Go back to the fish and tell him I want to be the controller of the sun and moon.'

The man was still half asleep but he was so horrified that he fell out of the bed. He thought he was having a nightmare and said, 'Wife, what are you saying?'

'Husband, if I can't be the controller of the universe I can't bear it, I shall never have another peaceful moment!'

He fell on his knees before her. 'Hear me, wife, the fish can't do that.'

Then she fell into a rage and her hair flew wildly about her head, she tore at her nightdress, kicked him and screamed, 'I can't stand it, I can't stand it any longer! Will you go this instant!' And he pulled on his trousers and ran off like a madman.

Outside a great storm was blowing so hard he could scarcely keep his feet. Houses and trees toppled over, the mountains trembled, rocks rolled into the sea. Down at the shore the waves were high as tower blocks and it was so dark he could hardly see the difference between heaven and earth. He cried out but could not hear his own words:

King Fish in the sea
Please listen to me
For my wife won't let things be
As I'd like them to be!

Through the storm he heard the fish say, 'Well, fisherman, what does she want now?'

'She wants to be the controller of the universe.'

'Go back,' said the fish. 'She's back in the shed already.'

In Asia, on the far side of the world it was a lovely day. A gentle wind blew, the clouds formed and sweet rain fell. The little fishing family went outside and the children played in the rain.

As for the fisherman and his wife in Norway, if they're not dead, they are still living in the shed.

Silence. The *Natural Storyteller* (you) finishes their story and then waits. Lets it sink in. A story is a seed that has been planted. It needs time to grow.

Living Water

This happened so long ago that the cedar, the fir and the pine trees still had needles that went yellow like other leaves and dropped in the autumn instead of staying green all winter.

In those olden times a man of the Tofalar people went out into the woods to hunt. He walked until he had walked further than any hunter had dared to go. He saw a wide, wet bog.

And he said to himself, 'This bog is huge. Animals can't run across this bog, and birds cannot fly across it, so what kinds of animals and birds live on the other side?'

The more he thought about it, the more curious he became. 'I must find out,' he said to himself. 'Whatever happens, I must get there.'

So he took a good running start and leapt clear across the bog.

He looked around and saw the same earth, the same water, the same grass, the same trees.

'Silly!' he said. 'There was no need to jump.'

Suddenly his mouth dropped open with wonder.

In a little clearing stood seven harnessed rabbits. They stood quietly, waiting. Then seven people came out of seven burrows in the earth, exactly like other people, only tiny. When the rabbits flattened their ears, the people were taller than the rabbits. When the rabbits' ears stood up, the people were smaller than the rabbits.

'Who are you?' asked the Tofalar.

'We are immortal people. We live for ever,' said the tiny men. 'We wash ourselves in living water and we never die. And who are you?'

'I am a hunter.'

The little men clapped their hands with joy.

'Oh, goody, goody!' they cried in chorus.

And one of them, the eldest, with white hair and a long white beard, came forward and said, 'A terrible, huge beast has come into our land. We don't know where it came from. The other day it caught one of our people and killed him. We are immortal, we are not supposed to die, but this beast killed one of us. You are a hunter – can you help us in this trouble? Can you hunt down the beast?'

'Why not?' answered the Tofalar, but to himself he wondered, 'Will I be able to kill such a frightful beast?'

However he went out to track the monster. He looked and he looked, but could find nothing except rabbits' footprints. Suddenly, among the rabbit prints he noticed the track of a little weasel smaller than a cat.

'Oh, that's too fine to miss,' he said. 'First I will get the weasel, and then I'll go on looking for the terrible, huge beast.'

He hunted and killed the weasel. Then he skinned it and went on with his search. He walked the length and breadth of the little people's land, but could not find any trace of the beast.

So he came back to the little people and said to them, 'I could not find your terrible, huge beast. All I have found was this weasel.' And he showed them the little weasel skin.

That's it, that's it!' they cried. 'Ooh, what a huge skin! What thick paws! What terrible, sharp claws!' And the eldest of the little men said to the Tofalar, 'You have saved us and our people! And we shall pay for your kindness with kindness. Wait for us. We'll come and bring you living water. You'll wash in it and live for ever.'

The Tofalar jumped back across the bog and went back to his valley and told his people about the little men.

The Tofalars began to wait for their guests, the immortal little people. They waited one day, three days, then many, many days. But the guests did not come and the Tofalars forgot about them and their promise. Winter came. Everything around was frozen. And the bog was covered with a coat of ice.

One day the women went to the woods to gather firewood. Suddenly a little herd of rabbits came galloping their way. They saw that every rabbit was saddled, and in every saddle sat a tiny man with a little bucket in his hands. The women burst out laughing at the sight.

'Look, look!' they cried to one another. 'They are riding on rabbits!'

'Look at the little men! How funny!'

'Oh, I'll die laughing!'

Now, the immortal people are a proud race. They were very offended at being laughed at. The one in front, with white hair and a long beard, shouted something to the others, and all of them spilled out the contents of their pitchers onto the ground. Then the rabbits turned and hopped away so fast that you could only see their white tails flicker.

So the Tofalars never got the living water. The living water went to the pine tree, the cedar and the fir. And this is why they are fresh and green all through the year. Their needles never die.

True or False?

1. The Tofalar hunter jumped over a bog.
2. The little people were riding on eagles.
3. They begged the hunter to kill a monster.
4. Living water is always fizzy and you must drink it through a pink straw.
5. The immortal people were giants.
6. The living water went to the pine tree, the cedar and the fir.

Myths from the Land of You

Invent a fantastical story that explains something in nature.
For example, why are daffodils yellow or how did the first fish
learn to swim?

Dolphin Friends

It's become popular for people in many parts of the world to swim out to sea and meet dolphins and whales. I know a woman called Amanda Stafford who has worked with dolphins for over twenty years. She says the sea animals seem always ready to connect to us. Sometimes people are astonished to find a dolphin looking them right in their eyes. Sometimes they play and imitate the humans in the sea. She says that when she meets dolphins she rediscovers her sense of humour and sometimes starts singing. Many people find this meeting with the sea creatures helps them rediscover what's really important in their lives. Here is a story about people in Australia who lived with the dolphins.

Gowanda was a respected elder who was big and strong with long white hair. He had many beloved hunting dogs. At his call his dogs would round up wallaby and kangaroo and drive them towards the hunters. Eventually Gowanda grew old and died, and his people were very sad.

One day some children playing on the beach saw a dolphin with a white fin swimming in the waves very close to the shore. They immediately recognised him. It was their beloved Gowanda. He had returned as a dolphin and in place of his long white hair he had a white fin. Just as he had taught his dogs to hunt, he was teaching other dolphins to round up the fish and drive them to shore for his people.

For children, dolphins now meant safety, as Gowonda and the other dolphins protected them from sharks while they were swimming. Since then, dolphins have had a very special relationship with the Yugambeh people of the Gold Coast. Among every school of dolphins, the ones with white fins are the leaders; they are Gowanda's great-grandchildren.

The River

Salmon and dolphins migrate over large distances but there have always been people who have done the same. When I was young I used to dream about being a Gypsy and roaming around with a horse and cart. Recently I got to know two beautiful young women from the Norwegian Romani people. They have their own secret language and have kept storytelling when many people have forgotten how to do it. In the Romani stories nature is truly alive. This is one of the tales I have told with them.

A Romani woman lived beside the emerald river. She loved to live in that place and she had everything she needed but each evening she sat on the river bank, cried salt tears and said, 'Oh river, how lucky I am to live beside your emerald waters. But one thing I lack. I wish I had a child to share this with.'

One evening, from the river bed she heard a deep melodious voice: 'I hear you.'

She looked out over the sparkling water and saw a little basket floating down the current. She pulled up her skirts, waded into the river and discovered the bright eyes of a baby in the basket. At once she knew this was her child and the river was his father.

As the baby grew he began to paddle in the water, then to swim and fish. On his fifth birthday his mother cut a stick and made him a little flute. He was soon trilling music with the melodious sounds of the river.

Happy years passed until one day the boy saw his mother sitting and crying salt tears into the river. 'Mum, what happened?' he asked.

'My son, yesterday a fortune-teller passed by. Recently I have been feeling weak so I asked her to tell my fortune. She threw down bones to see the future and told me that I won't live long. She has given me three gifts, a red scarf, a bucket and a young horse, but she says she can't help me more.'

'I will help you!' cried the boy. Then he turned to the river and called out, 'Emerald River, you are my father. Help us. Mother is terribly sick. What shall I do?'

Once again the deep voice resounded from the river bed: 'My child, there is one thing you can do, but it is a long and dangerous journey. You must travel upstream along my banks until you come to the place where I divide into five smaller streams.

One stream is white and one stream is grey,
The third stream is blue like the sky at midday,
The fourth stream is black and dark as the night
And the fifth stream is green and shining so bright.

'One of these streams leads to two steep mountains. These mountains are so much in love with one another that they kiss each other all day long. Beneath them is a spring. Their love is so strong and so pure that this spring water will cure any sickness in the world. But beware, my child, for the mountains guard this water jealously.'

The boy hugged his mother and, taking the scarf and bucket, jumped onto the horse and galloped along the riverbank. Soon he came to the place where the river divided into five streams.

One stream was white and one stream was grey,
The third stream was blue like the sky at midday,
The fourth stream was black and dark as the night
And the fifth stream was green and shining so bright.

Which stream should he follow? He had no idea. As he often did when he was confused, he took out his flute and began to play. Soon he heard a lovely voice singing. It didn´t sound like the river singing, but he saw no one else. So he and his horse jumped over the white stream, then jumped over the grey. They jumped over the blue stream like the sky at midday. They jumped over the stream as dark as the night and came to the green stream shining so bright. There beside this stream was a girl with black hair that was so long it flowed down along the waters of the brook. Her voice was so lovely that for a moment the boy forgot his worries and his urgent task. But when she stopped singing he said, 'Please tell me, have you ever heard of the two mountains who love each other so much they kiss all day long?'

'Yes,' said the girl. ´I was there when I was young. But I can't show you the way now. My hair has grown so long that as soon as I start walking it gets caught up in every bush or tree I pass by. Only here by the river can I relax and the river keeps my hair untangled.'

Suddenly the boy had an idea. He took the red scarf from the fortune-teller and wound it carefully around the girl's hair so that she could walk without getting her hair tangled.

'Thank you, thank you!' she said and jumped up on the horse to show him the way.

As they rode along the stream they spoke about the joys and the hardships of life so that it seemed like no time at all before they had reached the two towering mountains. Never before had the boy seen such a wonder – two mountains embracing one another passionately and he could feel the love radiating around the valley.

'Dear friend,' said the girl, 'there is a magic spring there between these mountains. But you must stay well away from there. Anyone who tries to get this water is crushed between the rocks.'

'One thing you must understand,' said the boy. 'I am as full of love for my mother as those two mountains are for one another. She has become very ill and I must get this water or die in the attempt.'

At that same moment they both had an idea. The girl took the bucket and plaited it into the horse's tail. Then she jumped back up onto the horse and began to sing and the boy to play his flute. As the sound of this wonderful music flowed out over the valley the two mountains relaxed their embrace and turned to see where the music was coming from. In that moment they galloped, still singing, towards the spring. The horse skilfully dipped its tail down to fetch the water and they rode away in the twinkling of an eye.

At that moment the mountains awakened from the music and with renewed passion crashed their rocky sides together again.

'We must hurry back to my mother,' called the boy and they galloped down the valley. As they approached they saw his mother lying lifeless on the river bank. At once they gave her a sip of water and she began to recover.

'My darling son, thank you,' she said. 'But who is this girl?'

'It's thanks to her we have got this medicine,' said her son.

'But why is she wearing the red scarf?'

'Don't you see? That's the scarf the fortune-teller gave you.'

'Son, you should know. It's the custom for us Gypsy women to wear a scarf when we marry.'

'Well in that case,' said the boy, 'I will ask her to marry me at once!'

At this the girl went quite pink and said yes.

What a wedding it was; I wish you had been there! The music was lovelier than a royal marriage. The river rippled its most splendid songs, and was joined by both the girl singing and the boy with his flute. All the local Romani people came with their horses, the fortune-teller brought many merry games, the horses galloped happily around them and the mother cried salt tears of joy by the lovely flowing waters.

Story Skeleton

To remember the river – seven things or characters in the story, then seven actions, then seven feelings. This is mine ...

7 nouns (things or characters)	7 verbs (actions)	7 feelings
River	Crying	Loneliness
Baby in a basket	Speaking	Joy
Flute	Playing music	Fear
Fortune-teller	Looking into the future	Courage
Girl with very long hair	Riding	Will
Mountains	Kissing	Understanding
Water of life	Dancing	Love

Cleaning the River

The First Nations people called the Salish have many traditions that honour the salmon and the river. They believe that salmon are full of wisdom and voluntarily agreed to give their bodies to us humans at the beginning of time when we were starving. In return, we need to do certain things to show them respect. One is to return the bones to the river. Another thing is never to fish too many fish, so that they can survive, spread and grow.

Another sign of respect is to keep the river clean. Perhaps you don't live near the sea but you almost certainly live not too far from a river, lake or stream. Often bits of plastic get washed into streams and rivers and end up in the sea. As you probably know, many birds and fish think the plastic looks like food, they eat it, it causes them suffering and many die.

If you feel like the Salish, that you would like to clean a river or stream, it's a good idea to get some gloves. Then go out with a big plastic bag and collect whatever rubbish you see. Before you go, let your adults know what you are planning and who you will be with. There may well be organised days where others in your local area are clearing plastic and this can happen anywhere, not just beside a river. The most important things to remove are plastic or batteries or other things that might be poisonous to fish and birds. Things like paper and food will rot away. The sooner you get rid of the plastic, the less likely it is to be eaten by living things.

This activity is double nice! You are helping the wildlife but also making the river a lovelier place for people to walk and for you and other children to play.

Did you solve the riddles?

Riddle 1:

What always runs but never walks,

Often murmurs, never talks,

Has a bed but never sleeps,

Has a mouth but never eats?

Riddle 2:

As I was going o'er London Bridge,

I heard something crack;

Not a man in all England

Can mend that.

Riddle 3:

What lives without breath,

Is cold as death?

Moving around,

It wears chain mail without a sound?

The answers are:
Riddle 1. A river.
Riddle 2. Ice.
Riddle 3. Fish.

Story Weather

Without the sky, the fiery sun, the drenching rains and cooling winds, this earth of ours would be a miserable home for us and the rest of nature. How do you talk about something this massive and mighty?

The sky is BIG, so let's start with some small riddles:

Riddle 1:

A house full, a hole full,

You cannot gather a bowl full.

Riddle 2:

At night they come without being fetched and in the morning they go

without being stolen. Higher than a house, higher than a tree,

oh, whatever can they be?

Riddle 3:

What cries without a voice,

Flies without wings,

Bites without teeth

And whispers but never sings

The Wind and the Sun

I heard this from my mum. It was first told by a slave in Greece called Aesop. They say he was so incredibly ugly that he became a great story-teller to survive. Recently, I was collecting stories from Afghans living in Oslo, and a woman told me the same fable. She didn't know about Aesop; she said it was an Afghan story. This is her version ...

The wind and the sun were up in the sky above the mountains of Afghanistan arguing about who was the strongest. Below them a traveller was hurrying down a rocky road, and the wind said, 'For goodness' sake, it's obvious I am stronger. We can have a competition. Whichever of us makes that traveller take off her big black chador wins. I start.'

So the sun hid behind a cloud, and the wind began to blow as hard as he could. The harder he puffed and blew with all his might, the more tightly the traveller wrapped her chador round her body, till at last the wind gave up, exhausted.

Then the sun emerged from behind the cloud. It was shining gloriously and the traveller, tired after the terrible tussle, was soon so hot she threw off her chador and lay joyfully on a soft grassy bank.

You have almost reached the last section of the Natural Storyteller. *I really hope you have been enjoying it. One of the main things about a* Natural Storyteller *is that they relish the stories. Some people listen or read stories for years before they tell them. This way they get to live inside you and grow. The story seeds are planted and grow slow and well. You've got your whole life ahead of you; you don't need to tell any stories now. But the more you dream about them the better they will be planted for the day you do want to tell them, maybe only for yourself. If you are sitting on a bus, a car or your bed, bored out of your mind, try this. Settle into your own private screening – project your own film of a story in your mind-cinema.*

Gluscabi and the Wind Eagle

Once there was a boy called Gluscabi, who lived with his grandfather and grandmother in a lodge beside a lake. One day Grandfather and Gluscabi found a tree trunk lying on the forest floor. Grandfather took his axe and hollowed out a canoe from the tree.

'This is for you, Grandson,' he said.

Gluscabi sploshed the canoe onto the lake and began to paddle out onto the water. As he paddled he felt on top of the world and sang:

Paddling on the lake, silver and blue,
Nobody has seen such a cool canoe!
Look at me, look at me,
Doobedoobedoo!

All of a sudden a wind blew up and blew and blew Gluscabi and his canoe all the way back to shore. But Gluscabi didn't give up. Once again he paddled out and this time he sang his song a little louder:

PADDLING ON THE LAKE, SILVER AND BLUE,
NOBODY HAS SEEN SUCH A COOL CANOE!
LOOK AT ME, LOOK AT ME,
DOOBEDOOBEDOO!

But again the wind came and blew him right back to shore. Four times he tried to paddle out into the lake and four times he failed.

Gluscabi went back to the lodge of his grandmother and walked right in, even though there was a stick leaning across the door, which meant that Grandmother was doing some work and did not want to be disturbed.

'Grandmother,' said Gluscabi, 'what makes the wind blow?'

Grandmother Woodchuck looked up from her work. 'Gluscabi,' she said, 'why do you want to know?'

'Because,' he said.

Grandmother Woodchuck looked at him. 'Ah, Gluscabi,' she said, 'whenever you ask such questions I feel there is going to be trouble. Perhaps I should not tell you. But I know that you are very stubborn and will never stop asking. So, I shall tell you. If you walk facing into the wind you will come to the place where Wuchowsen the wind eagle stands.'

'Thank you, Grandmother!' said Gluscabi. He stepped out of the lodge, faced into the wind and began to walk.

He walked over meadows, he jumped over streams, he trotted through woods and the wind blew hard. He swam over rivers, walked through valleys and into the hills and the wind blew harder. He came to the foothills and began to climb and the wind blew harder still.

The foothills were becoming mountains and the wind was very strong. Soon there were no longer any trees and the wind was even stronger.

The wind was so strong that it blew off Gluscabi's moccasins. But he was very stubborn and he kept on walking, leaning into the wind. Now the wind was so strong that it blew off his shirt, but he was so stubborn that he kept on walking. Now the wind was so strong that it blew off his trousers and he was naked! But he was very stubborn and kept on walking.

The wind was so strong it even blew off his hair, but Gluscabi kept walking, facing into the wind. The wind was so strong that it blew off his eyebrows, but still he continued to walk.

Now the wind was so strong that he could not stand. He lay down and pulled himself along by grabbing hold of the boulders. There, on the peak ahead of him, he could see a great bird flapping its wings. It was Wuchowsen, the wind eagle.

Gluscabi took a deep breath. 'GRANDFATHER!' he shouted.

The wind eagle stopped flapping his wings and looked around. 'Who calls me Grandfather?' he said.

Gluscabi stood up. 'It's me, Grandfather. I came up here to tell you that you are doing a great job making the wind blow.'

The wind eagle puffed out his chest with pride. 'You mean like this?' he said and he flapped his wings even harder. The wind that he made was so strong that it lifted Gluscabi right off his feet, and he would have been blown right off the mountain had he not reached out and grabbed a boulder.

'GRANDFATHER!!!' Gluscabi shouted again.

The wind eagle stopped flapping his wings. 'Yes?' he said.

Gluscabi stood up and came closer to Wuchowsen. 'You do a great job making the wind blow, Grandfather. But you could do an even better job if you were on that peak over there.'

The wind eagle looked over towards the other mountain peak. 'Maybe,' he said, 'but how would I get over there?'

Gluscabi smiled. 'Grandfather,' he said, 'I will carry you. Wait here.'

Gluscabi ran back down the mountain until he came to a big basswood tree. He stripped off the outer bark and from the inner bark he braided a strong carrying strap which he took back up the mountain to the wind eagle.

'Here, Grandfather,' he said. 'I will wrap this around you so I can lift you easily.' Then he wrapped the carrying strap so tightly around Wuchowsen that his wings were pulled into his sides and he could hardly breathe.

'Now, Grandfather,' said Gluscabi, picking the wind eagle up, 'I will take you to the other peak.'

He began to walk towards the other peak, but as he walked he came to a large crevice, and as he stepped over it he let go of the carrying strap and the wind eagle slid down into the crevice, upside down, and was stuck.

'Huh!' said Gluscabi. 'It is time to go paddle my canoe.'

He walked back down the mountain and there was no wind at all. He walked till he came to the treeline and still no wind blew. He walked down to the foothills and down to the hills and the valleys, he swam the river, walked through the forest, jumped the stream, crossed over the meadows and the wind did not blow at all.

He got back to the lodge by the water and by now all his hair had grown back.

He put on some fine new clothes and a new pair of moccasins and went back to the water and climbed into his canoe.

He paddled out into the water and sang:

Paddling on the lake, silver and blue!
Nobody has seen such a cool canoe!
Look at me, look at me,
Doobedoobedoo!

The air was very warm and Gluscabi began to sweat. It was still and hot and it was hard to breathe. Soon the water began to smell so rotten that he could hardly paddle. The fishes were gasping for air on the surface of the water and the birds were so warm they could no longer fly in the air.

Gluscabi returned to the shore and went straight to his grandmother's lodge and walked in.

'Grandmother,' he said, 'what is wrong? The air is hot and still and it is making me sweat and it is hard to breathe. The water is smelly and I cannot paddle in my canoe like this.'

Grandmother Woodchuck looked up at Gluscabi. 'Gluscabi,' she said, 'what have you done now?'

And Gluscabi answered, 'Oh, nothing.'

'Gluscabi,' said Grandmother Woodchuck again, 'tell me what you have done.'

Then Gluscabi told her about going to visit the wind eagle and what he had done to stop the wind.

'Oh, Gluscabi,' said Grandmother Woodchuck.

'The Creator set Wuchowsen the wind eagle on the mountain for a reason. Wuchowsen makes wind to keep the air clean. Wind brings clouds that give us rain to wash the earth, to keep it fresh and sweet. Without the wind, life will be bad for us, for our children, and our children's children. Bad for us, bad for the fish, the birds, the beasts. This wind is the breath of the world.'

Gluscabi nodded his head. 'Grandmother,' he said, 'I understand.'

He went outside. He faced in the direction where the wind had once blown and began to walk.

He walked over meadows, he jumped over streams, he trotted through woods and the wind did not blow and he was very hot. He swam over rotting rivers, walked into the hills and there was no wind and it was very hard to breathe. But Gluscabi was stubborn and he began to climb the foothills.

Now the foothills became mountains and he was so hot and sweaty he could hardly stagger along. But Gluscabi was very stubborn and somehow he did not give up. He was very scared, thinking the wind eagle might have died in that crack in the rock.

At last he came to the mountain and he looked down into the crevice. There was Wuchowsen, the wind eagle, wedged upside down, as still as a stone.

'Uncle?' Gluscabi called.

He heard a weak voice: 'Who calls me Uncle?'

'It is Gluscabi, Uncle. I'm up here. But what are you doing down there?'

'Oh, Gluscabi,' said the wind eagle, 'an ugly, naked boy with no hair told me that he would take me to the other peak so that I could do a better job of making the wind blow. He tied my wings and picked me up, but as he stepped over this crevice he dropped me in and I am stuck. And I am not comfortable here at all.'

'Ah, Grandfath . . . er, Uncle, I will get you out.'

Then Gluscabi climbed down into the crevice. He pulled the wind eagle free, placed him back on the mountain and untied his wings.

'Uncle,' Gluscabi said, 'maybe the wind should blow sometimes and other times not.'

The wind wagle looked at Gluscabi and then nodded his head. 'Grandson,' he said, 'I hear what you say.'

And so that story goes.

When a *Natural Storyteller* is telling a tale do they move their arms? The answer is yes and, then again, no. Some of them are like TUUP (his full title is The Unprecedented Unorthodox Preacher), who started telling stories with me in West London in the beginning of time. He flows around like the wind blowing here there and everywhere and moves not only his arms but his whole body and voice. But some are like the blind storyteller I heard in Ireland who hardly moved a muscle and yet everyone in that tiny pub was utterly spellbound. See the story and it will live through you and your body – naturally.

Harvesting the Sky

Some people want to release less carbon dioxide because of climate change.
They have stopped using ordinary electricity. Here are their stories.

Maxine and Don live in Canada. They harvest the sky in two ways. They soak up sunshine with their solar panels and they collect big stacks of pinewood. Not far from their cabin are lots of pine trees that have been grown from the sunshine, then been killed by beetles so they are just lying on the forest floor. Dan and Maxine chop the logs out in the forest, lift them onto their truck, drive home, cut the wood to size, bring it indoors and put it in their stove. So it's quite a lot of work, but all the work makes them warm so they don't need so much heating!

Burning wood in a stove can get very hot very quickly so they have made a huge water battery where they store the heat. The fire warms up 24,000 litres (300 bathtubs) of water, which they keep in plastic containers. This warm water makes their house stay cosy much longer. They didn't buy new plastic containers, as that would add to carbon dioxide emissions, so they went to schools, restaurants and recycling depots and collected containers that had been used for soap, wax, laundry detergent and soy sauce.

During autumn and spring they don't need the wood stove. Warm air is fanned down from the solar collector on their roof by their old car heater-blower, and heat gets stored in their water-filled containers.

Linn and Mike live in another house in Canada shaped like a dome. They have laid 18,00 blocks under the floor. The sun shines onto the floor which acts as a battery to store the warmth. At night, they close the shutters to keep the heat inside. They have built their dome house with many windows on the south side, the side where the sun shines most, so they can get as much solar heat and light as possible.

These people who have decided to make all their own light and warmth are called 'Off-Gridders'. There are many people who try not to waste electricity and make as much as they can of their own. Conrad and his wife and two children don't have a car. They cycle everywhere. They have a cycle trailer if they need to carry any big bits of wood home for the stove. They live very far north, so it can be pretty cold, but still their stove and solar panels mean they only use ordinary electricity for ten per cent of the time.

These families think it's a bit boring to live in the same temperature day in day out. They enjoy feeling the difference between heat and cold.

Myths from the Land of You

In stories things usually go very wrong before they go right again. Imagine a family who decide to save as much electricity as possible. It's so hard and so difficult they almost give up but then something happens to make them realise that they can have fun doing it. And they all live happily ever after.

Before you start to tell a story it's not a bad idea to breathe. Maybe ask your listeners a question or tell them where you heard this story, or something. Just so you can have a look at them and they can have a look at you before you launch into your story. Breathe again and off you go ...

Snow

There was once a mother who had two girls and they lived together in the forest under the blue skies and the dark storms. In this family the older daughter did all the work.

She went out and found dead trees lying on the forest floor, dragged them home and chopped them up to keep the house warm. Meanwhile her younger sister sat by the fire, moaning that it was too cold. The older sister took the sheep out onto the windswept moor to munch on grass and nettles. Then in the springtime, when their coats were long and woolly, she took sharp sheep shears and clipped the wool off to make clothes. She herself never got new clothes but only the worn-out old dresses the others didn't want.

One spring morning she went out into the sunshine. First she gave the sheep their morning hug, for they were her best friends. Then she took her sharp shears and cut off their wool, and the sheep were so happy to get out of their heavy winter clothes they sprang round in a ring. Then the sky darkened and it started bucketing down with rain.

'Mum, can I come in now?' the girl called in through the window.

'Certainly not. First you must spin all the wool into thread, lazy girl!'

So she took the spinning wheel out under a tree and began to spin. She spun and spun until there was a huge pile of woollen thread and her fingers got so sore that blood ran down onto the earth.

'Mum, can I come in now?' the girl called in through the window.

'Certainly not. That blood will turn the wool red. Go and spin by the well, lazy girl!'

So in the drizzling rain she sat by the well and spun, and every now and then washed the spindle in the well water.

'Mmmmmaaaa!' called the sheep as if to comfort her. The day wore on and the rain fell and the heap of wool was still higher than she was. At last she leaned once more into the well to wash the spindle and it slipped out of her hand and dropped down into the water.

'Mum, I dropped the spindle down the well,' the girl called in through the window.

'Jump down and get it out, you lazy girl!'

So she did. She climbed onto the well wall, shut her eyes and jumped. Plunging into the icy water and falling down, down, down into the darkness. When she opened her eyes she found herself in a beautiful meadow. The sun shone bright, the birds sang like a happy orchestra and yellow butterflies danced over the flowers. For a moment she lay on the warm, sweet-smelling grass. Then she heard, 'Help us! Help us! We are burning!'

She jumped up. The voices seemed to cry out from a large round oven steaming in the grass. She opened the oven door. Inside she saw rows of delicious-smelling loaves of bread, so she took the bread shovel and drew out them out. Then she heard hundreds of little voices calling, 'Help! Pick us! We're ripe!'

The voices seemed to come from a large tree covered with red apples. So she picked the apples and laid them under the tree. Beside the tree was a house. Leaning out of the window was a tremendously ugly old lady.

'Can you help me? Please I do need help!'

'What do you need help with?'

'This and that, but the most important thing is that you shake out my duvet so the people in the world above will have snow.'

The girl swept and cleaned and gave the duvet a proper shake every day until the feathers flew around like snowflakes. As she worked the old lady cooked tasty food and let her eat as much as she wanted. The old lady also told jokes and sang in a croaky old voice and the girl had a lovely time. But one morning she said, 'Dear old lady, it's so cosy living here with you. I don't understand why, but I am homesick.'

'My dear, it's only natural that you should miss your own family,' said the old woman. 'What a help you have been to me. The way home is straight through that archway.'

At the bottom of the garden the girl saw a curving arch she had never noticed before, with yellow sweet fragrant flowers growing around it. So she gave the old lady a big hug and walked through. As she stepped under the arch she felt as if a golden sun was pouring over her. Looking down, she saw to her amazement that all her clothes had transformed into pure gold. Her skin was gold. Her hair was gold. Even her fingernails were gold. Oh, she was shining like a little sun herself. And there, straight ahead of her, was her own house. She skipped up to the house and ran inside.

There sat her mother and sister miserably in front of the fire which had gone out. They stared at her and then to her astonishment they asked her to sit down on the sofa and made her tea and bread and jam. Life was much nicer for her now, but they were very curious and asked her where she had been and how she had come to be so golden.

Then the younger sister said, 'Mum, it's not fair, I want to be golden too.'

'What are you waiting for?' said the mum.

So the younger sister went over to the well. She couldn't be bothered to do any spinning, so she pricked her finger with the spindle and chucked it down the well. Then she jumped down. Down into the icy water she fell and when she opened her eyes she was lying on warm grass in the meadow. The sun shone, the birds sang like a happy orchestra and yellow butterflies danced over the flowers.

She heard voices: 'Help us! Help us! We are burning!'

She jumped up. The voices came from the oven steaming in the grass. She opened the oven door and shouted, 'You stupid bread! Do you think I'm going to burn my fingers on you? No chance!'

Then she heard hundreds of little voices calling, 'Help! Pick us! We're ripe!'

The voices came from the large apple tree.

'Why should I pick you, silly apples? What have you ever done for me? One of you might fall on my head!'

Beside the tree was the house and leaning out of the window was the tremendously ugly old lady.

'Can you help me? It's terribly important.'

'Oh yes, I'm fantastic at helping.'

'Very well, please remember you must shake out my duvet so the people in the world above will have snow.'

'Of course.'

The first day, the younger sister worked hard. She swept the floor and wiped the table and shook the duvet so that the feathers flew about like snowflakes. That night she was very tired, as she wasn't used to working, so the next day she woke up late and didn't do much.

The third day, she stayed in bed all day.

'I'm sorry, my dear,' said the old lady, 'but you're not doing the work; you'll have to go home.' This was just what the girl had been waiting for and without another word she ran down the garden just as her sister had said.

As she walked through the archway a very strange feeling came over her. As if a bucket of slime had been poured all over her. It was cold and wet and she ran into her house screaming. When her mother and sister saw her they screamed too. She was covered in disgusting stuff, like smelly poo.

It took a long time to clean it all off. But the older sister felt sorry for her and helped her. One day the little sister only had a few blobs of disgusting slime left on her and the two of them went to the river and swam. The little sister laughed and they played and played. When she got out of the river all the slime was gone. When they got home instead of moaning and shouting at them for being late their mum had made a delicious dinner of pancakes.

I can't promise they were nice every single day but they did become kinder as the years went by. And that way they also got happier!

This is an old story. Like most people in history this family had no water in their home. They needed to fetch water from a well. In many parts of the world it's still like that and some people, often women and children, have to go far to collect water.

Have you ever fetched water from a well? You have to be very careful. If by mistake you fall down a well you will need help to get out or you might drown. But water brings life, especially if there is little rain. A good well is a blessing and there are many, many fairytales and legends about wells.

Rain Magic

Not so long ago, people all over the world used magic to try and control the sky.

For example, in a village in Russia, when rain was needed, three men used to climb up the fir trees of an old sacred grove. Once up in the tree, one of them drummed with a hammer on a kettle to imitate thunder. The second knocked two burning sticks together and made the sparks fly to imitate lightning; and the third man, who was called 'the rain-maker', had a bunch of twigs which he dipped in a pot to sprinkle water. This was to bring rain. Recently I was in Estonia and I was amazed to be shown a tree where three men climbed up and did almost exactly the same thing!

When it was terribly dry in a village in Ukraine, women and girls would go naked by night to the boundaries of the village and pour water on the ground. They said this could help bring rain.

Some people think this is just old-fashioned superstition, while others, like myself, may have had an experience to make them wonder if people can sometimes change the weather. A few years ago I was staying in a Tibetan monastery in India and they were preparing the biggest celebration of the year. Every year they have a massive party and invite people from miles around. They eat outside and watch dancers swirling around dressed as demons and gods.

The trouble was the weather was terrible. There were very unseasonal huge storms every day and lots of rain. At last the morning of the party arrived; we went outside and saw the sky was clear and blue. Far up on the monastery wall was the abbot waving at us to come up.

When we had climbed up we said, 'How lucky that exactly today is so beautiful when all your guests will come.'

'Oh not lucky – hard work!' said the abbot laughing. 'I praying all night. Now you go party and I pray some more. Go enjoy Tibetan New Year!'

Sun Magic

Today we have weather scientists who warn us when there will be an eclipse blocking out the sun. In days gone by, an eclipse could be seen as a very worrying occurrence. The Ojibwe people in Canada used to worry that the sun was in danger of going out! So they shot fire-tipped arrows in the air to rekindle the sun's light. The Sencis of Peru also shot burning arrows at the sun during an eclipse; they said it was to drive away a savage beast that was fighting the sun. When there was an eclipse in Far East Russia the Kamtchatkan people brought out fire from their huts and prayed to the sun to shine as before. They were sure it worked because the sun began to shine again.

In ancient Egypt the king was seen to represent the sun, and he walked solemnly round the walls of the temple to make sure that the sun would perform his daily journey round the sky.

Wind Magic

Until about 1860 most ships used wind power to move over the oceans. Finnish wizards used to sell wind to sailors who needed it to sail their ships. They gave them a cloth which that three knots tied in it. If the sailor undid the first knot, it was said a moderate wind would spring up; if they untied the second knot, the wind blew half a gale; if the third, a hurricane!

People in Estonia used to say that the bitter winds that blow from the northeast, bringing illness with them, came from Finnish wizards and witches. A popular song ran,

Wind of the Cross! Rushing and mighty!
Heavy the blow of your wings sweeping past!
Wild wailing wind of misfortune and sorrow,
Wizards of Finland ride by on the blast.

The art of tying up the wind in three knots was popular with wizards and witches in many places. Shetland seamen would also buy winds in the shape of knotted handkerchiefs or threads from old women who claimed to rule the storms. Scottish witches used to raise the wind by dipping a rag in water and beating it three times on a stone, saying,

I knok this rag upone this stane
To raise the wind in the divellis name,
It sall not lye till I please againe.

In the famous Greek story of Odysseus, who struggled to get back home to his wife and son, he was given the winds in a leather bag by Aeolus, King of the Winds, to help him sail home.

Rain

The next story is from Zimbabwe. Often African stories contain one or more songs. When the listeners know the songs they join in during the story. So it's not like there is one storyteller and an audience; it's more like everyone is telling the story.

O nce there lived a boy who had no mother, no father, no sister and no brothers, so he lived out in the bush. He made friends with the animals and the birds but one day he stopped crawling and stood up on his two legs and suddenly felt alone. So he decided to travel over the bush to see if he could find some other two-legged creatures like himself.

He walked for three days and three nights until he came to a large village. As he entered the village in the early evening all heads turned towards him and they said, 'Who are you, stranger?' and he answered saying, 'My name is Chinemakuate – and I have come to help you if you need help.'

'Huh?' they said. 'We cannot afford help. Why do we need a strange boy? Go away.'

So the boy hung his head and walked alone through the village.

On the other side of the village, he saw the old people, the white-haired ones, sitting in the shade of a large tree and the chief of the village turned to him and said, 'Who are you?'

He said, 'My name is Chinemakuate, and I have come to help you if you need help.'

'Yes,' said the chief, 'you can be my herd-boy and you can live there.'

He pointed the boy in the direction of a simple hut and inside was an old woman and she said, 'Hallo, my name is Old-covered-in-ashes because I am

214

old and covered in ashes.' So the boy came in and she made food for him and it was the first time he had tasted food made by another human being and he was happy.

Early next morning Old-covered-in-ashes took him out into the early morning sun and he saw before him a huge herd of beautiful cows, their horns curving up to the heavens. But as he approached them he saw to his horror that all the beautiful cattle were so thin and bony that their bones were almost sticking out through their skin. He said, 'I am the new herd-boy of the chief. I will help you! I promise.'

He led them out far out into the bush but everywhere he looked to left and to right the grass was dried up and even the leaves on the trees were not fit for eating. At last he stopped in the desert and he saw that the cattle were so weak that they were trembling and shaking and some began to collapse. What could he do? What on earth could he do?

Chinemakuate climbed up onto a large rock and from deep inside himself he found a song:

Deyan deyan deyawe, Deyan deyan deya. Deyan deyan deyawe, Deyan deyan deya. Shimendewan dewa, shimendewan dewa. Shimendewan dewa, shimendewan dewa.

In the parched blue sky, the heavens darkened and from the clouds poured rain, cascading onto the backs of the cattle, who threw back their heads and mooed with pure delight. Beneath the earth hundreds and thousands of invisible seeds cracked open and began to grow. Every day the boy went back to that place and every day he sang until the whole place was sprouting and green.

Back in the village the old chief turned to the people and said, 'Who is this boy, this Chinemakuate?'

And they said, 'He is nobody, just a ragged stranger.'

But he said, 'No you are wrong. Look at how fat and well our cows are looking. Tomorrow I will follow him.'

So next day he followed him out into the bush and secretly watched. Then he brought him back into the village, put him up onto a large stone and said 'Sing!' and the boy sang:

Deyan deyan deyawe, Deyan deyan deya. Deyan deyan deyawe, Deyan deyan deya. Shimendewan dewa, shimendewan dewa. Shimendewan dewa, shimendewan dewa.

The sky darkened and blessed rain fell from the sky. All the children threw off their clothes and began to play in the water and the old people raised their faces to the heavens and thanked the Sky God that he had sent a ragged stranger boy to bring rain.

Make a Sky Story

Yes – without this sky up there, the burning sun, the rain cascading into the rivers and all those winds and breezes, this earth of ours would be no home for us and the rest of nature.

Let's pretend to be a magician and storyteller of our tribe. The people need a sky story to remember how great the sky really is.

1. First get yourself ready; maybe find a magic feather, a cloak to wear or something else to help. Perhaps you can make a flag to celebrate the weather.
2. Then, whatever the weather is, whether it's stormy, windy, drizzling or boiling hot, go outside. If it's chilly bring plenty of clothes or a blanket. Walk around and find a place where you can see the sky comfortably. Either sit, stand or lie down, and stay there quietly for a whole ten minutes, with your body feeling the weather, and looking at the sky. What colour is it really? Do you see any strange dots? Perhaps it's night and you can see some stars, or even imagine them during the day. Just be there in the weather for at least ten minutes.
3. If you are cold come inside; otherwise stay where you are, close your eyes and see if a weather or sky story comes into your mind. There are so many kinds of stories – find one you like. Perhaps it's a story that you already know but now you focus on the sky in the tale. Perhaps it's a story from this book which you make into your own version. Perhaps it's something that happened to you or someone you know which is to do with the sky. Perhaps it's something that just comes up in your imagination.
4. Now shut your eyes and try and see the whole story as if it's a film in your mind. You are the director of this film, it's up to you what it looks like. For now, don't tell yourself the story; just watch it as if you are there, taking in the atmosphere. Some people really enjoy doing this bit. Take as long as you want.
5. Then, take some coloured pencils and draw the whole thing. It doesn't matter

if it's a really terrible drawing. It's not for the National Gallery. It's just for you to remember the story.

6. Then ... tell someone. If there are no other two-legged animals around, tell it to your cat, your cuddly toy, a tree or to the thin air ...

7. Congratulations, you have just made a sky story!

Did you solve the riddles?

Riddle 1:

A house full, a hole full,

You cannot gather a bowl full.

Riddle 2:

At night they come without being fetched and in the morning they go

without being stolen. Higher than a house, higher than a tree,

oh, whatever can they be?

Riddle 3:

What cries without a voice,

Flies without wings,

Bites without teeth

And whispers but never sings

The answers are:
Riddle 1. Fog.
Riddle 2. Stars.
Riddle 3. Wind.

The First Party

Dear *Natural Storyteller* apprentice, you are nearing the end of this book.

If you have gleaned some joyful moments, or told at least one story to your cat, little brother or friend, you are on the path. It's a long and winding path and will require a lot of industry before you become a Master or Mistress *Natural Storyteller*. But once you have taken the first step along the path it will always be there for you.

One last piece of advice. Enjoy telling your story. As long as you enjoy the story you are telling, your listeners will surf on your enthusiasm and join you.

Two last riddles:

Riddle 1:

I can touch you but you can't touch me.

Although I have no wheels, wings or sails, I can take you on a long journey.

Sometimes you can see me best with your eyes closed! What am I?

Riddle 2:

I am not a tree but I was a tree.

I am not a person but yet I talk.

I am not a plant but I have leaves that some call pages.

I do not speak yet I can make you laugh.

What am I?

The First Party

Long ago people were always sad and serious. They had no jokes and never laughed. They had no birthday parties or Christmas, no Eid banquet, no weddings or even funerals. Life was just boring work and dreamless sleep and one day was exactly like the last. People often stared at birds singing and wondered why they always seemed so happy.

On the coast of Greenland lived a man and wife with their three sons. Every day they went hunting. One evening as they sat in utter silence as usual the father asked, 'Where is Big One?' (They didn't even have names; they were called Big One, Middle One and Small One.)

No one knew where Big One was and a few days later Middle One didn't come home either. The family went out to look but couldn't find them and felt sad. The parents tried to keep an eye on Small One but one day when he was out alone a huge eagle flew towards him. He took up his bow and was about to shoot. As it landed before him it transformed into a tall man with a sharp beaky nose.

'I have taken your brothers. We tried to give them the gift of party but they refused. Come with me or I will kill you too,' said Eagle-man. Small One didn't understand but he was both frightened and curious. He sat on Eagle-man's back up to the high mountain top. There, on a massive nest, sat old Eagle-mother. She looked tired and miserable. Her old beak pecked at her bedraggled feathers.

'Mother, at last I have found a human who will learn to party,' said Eagle-man. At that old Eaglemother perked up and they began to teach him at once. Small One didn't get it at all. He had never heard of singing, dancing, laughing or stories.

They worked both day and night, but still he was utterly useless at partying. When he sang it was so silly that the eagles laughed and when he tried to crack a joke it was so unfunny they cried.

'What is wrong with you, human child?' squawked Eagle-mother one day.

'I don't know. I keep thinking about Big One and Middle One who disappeared,' answered Small One.

'Ah, now I understand,' said the old eagle, 'Why didn't I think of this before?' So she taught him an ancient sorrowing song, to sing at a funeral for someone who has died. Suddenly Small One found a huge singing voice and began to howl and sing and cry aloud in honour of his two brothers.

After this he began to learn new songs. The song of remembering the dead, the song of welcoming new days, the song of thanking the parents, the song of anger and rage. And as he sang his body began to move. Then they taught him the dance of the new moon, the dance of the deer hunt and the dance of the girl's first kiss. One day to their utter surprise Small One told a joke and it was so funny the two eagles fell on their backs laughing. Still they had to teach him the recipes of feasting food and of building the party house but he had such fun learning he hardly noticed that a whole year had passed. Then they sent him home.

He returned to find his parents sitting silent as usual by the evening fire. They stared at him in disbelief and he began to sing, a warm and wondrous celebration song of reuniting. The tears poured down their cheeks. Then he went around all the houses in the area to invite everyone to the world's first human party.

As the days passed they packed snow to build the first meeting house. While cooking and practising dances and songs, they noticed something. Getting the party ready for the guests made them warm in their hearts. In the evenings normally they would have been so bored but now they sat together and chatted and joked.

At last the big day arrived. Guests arrived from south, north, east and west and crowded into the big meeting house. They were served masses of delicious food. Everyone learnt to sing and to dance and this extraordinary first party lasted all night. During the course of the night they gave Small One a new name – Weasel. Have you ever seen a weasel? They are such quick movers, maybe that's why he got his name.

In the early morning, as guests were hugging and laughing and thanking, Weasel watched them leave the house. A very strange thing happened – as they walked away some of them changed into reindeer, some became eagles or great white polar bears! He realised that some of their guests were animals and birds. A good party makes different animals seem the same.

It didn't take long before people found many new reasons to throw a party. A good harvest can be celebrated, or a new baby. When two young people want to spend their life together in love, dancing and presents seem natural. And in the midwinter, when everything is cold and dark, it can be extra nice to gather, eat good food and retell old stories …

One day Weasel walked up the mountain to meet Eagle-man and old Eagle-mother. He wanted to tell them about the very first party, about how everyone was teaching one another to sing, and most of all he wanted to thank them. When he finally got up to the Eagle nest he was so surprised to see old Eagle mother again. She was looking so young; her feathers were fluffy and her eyes sparkling! When people party, old eagles become young.

How did you get on with the riddles?

Riddle 1:

I can touch you but you can't touch me.

Although I have no wheels, wings or sails, I can take you on a long journey.

Sometimes you can see me best with your eyes closed! What am I?

Riddle 2:

I am not a tree but I was a tree.

I am not a person but yet I talk.

I am not a plant but I have leaves that some call pages.

I do not speak yet I can make you laugh.

What am I?

The answers are:
Riddle 1. You have just read about fifty of these things – a story! The answer could also be music.
Riddle 2. A clue ... you are nearly at the end of one.

Make a Story Party

Now you have read this book I hope you have found at least one story you really like. Maybe you want to tell it or maybe you want to listen to it. So now it's time for a story party. It can be just as big or as small as you want. If you have that kind of teacher you can ask to have a story party with your class or a younger class.

How to do it:

1. Invite some people! It could be your family, neighbours or friends. Ask everyone to bring something to eat or drink and to bring either a story to tell or some ears to listen with. A written invitation is usually extra effective.

2. Ask someone who is friendly and relaxed to be the host. You can do it yourself but you might want to sit back and enjoy it. The host will perhaps tell a short story or riddle to warm up the audience. Then they introduce people and encourage those who want to share a story.

3. Before the day of the party it's a good idea to ask a few people if they have thought of a story to tell. Maybe you know someone who you think is a great storyteller. You don't need a lot of stories but you need a few! If you ask people it also reminds them the party is coming up.

4. Make the party room ready by getting some cosy cushions and places to sit.

5. It can be nice to have music playing and people can chat as they arrive and have a drink. When they have arrived you might want to play a game to break the ice.

6. If it's a small group there may be a great atmosphere. If you have lots of people then, depending on how brave they are feeling, you can divide into smaller groups so people who feel shy don't need to tell their story to everyone at once. The host can introduce people and make them feel comfortable. Be a good listener yourself. If you are a really good listener then you make it much easier for the storytellers to get into their story.

7. After you have heard a few stories, maybe after about half an hour, the host can thank the tellers and announce it's time to eat. Now everyone has a chance to talk about the stories and chat.

8. Then, if there are a few more people with stories, it's time for part 2. If there's someone who would like to sing a song or play some music that will make a brilliant interlude. It can be too much with too many stories in one evening.

Did you manage all this? Then you have become a link in the chain in the oral tradition. Perhaps some of the stories told this night will never be forgotten.

Afterword

Georgiana and I have been telling stories for a long time. Back in the 1980s we used to perform together as part of a group called 'The Company of Storytellers'. If we were to add together the number of years we've earned our living as tellers, the total would be a whole lifetime, more than seventy years.

In all that time there has been one question that I find myself being asked over and over again. Teachers, parents, librarians and grown-ups of all kinds draw me quietly to one side after a performance and they say: 'These old traditional stories are all very well but they've got nothing to do with the way we live our lives today. Why aren't you telling stories about housing estates and computers and smart-phones? What have talking animals, fables and fairy-tales got to do with the real world of multinational companies, economic migrants and global warming? Isn't it time you started telling stories for *now*?'

It's a question that children never ask.

Maybe children instinctively recognise something that their elders have forgotten: that nothing has really changed. Just like our ancestors, we still depend for our survival on the generosity of the land. We may no longer be surrounded by farms and fields and forests but our lives are interwoven with the lives of insects, plants, animals and birds. Their well-being is our well-being. The elemental energies of fire, water, air and earth are as crucial to us as they have ever been. We live out our lives under sun, moon and stars. And emotionally we are no different – greed, kindness, anger, courage, jealousy, love, laziness, laughter and sorrow inhabit us, just as they inhabited our great-, great-, great-, great-grandfathers and grandmothers.

This is the stuff of story. It may be at one remove from the familiar modern world but its ingredients are as true as they've ever been.

The difference between us and those ancestors who first found the stories is that we are no longer aware that we are dependent on nature. For them, a moment of greed or thoughtlessness might have led directly to hunger or disease. They had to live in a right relationship with their world in order to survive. We have become blind to those connections but they are no less true for being out of sight.

The stories that our ancestors told remind us that we are all part of an organic whole. Everything is reciprocal. Animals, fishes, birds and plants are endlessly generous in their gift of themselves ... but there are conditions, and the central one is that we, as fellow creatures, must never forget that we are members of the same sprawling family.

If we're looking for stories for *now*, these must be the ones!

In *The Natural Storyteller* Georgiana retells traditional stories from many cultures. All of them explore themes of interdependence and sustainability (and there are some beauties – 'The Birch Tree' and 'The King of the Deer' are two of my favourites). But what makes her book unique is that her years of working as a storyteller give it a sense of adventure and fun. She knows how to talk with children. She is chatty and engaging. The book is a journey into storytelling as well as story. There are lots of tips about how to remember the structure of a story. She understands that once a story is learnt it actually works its way into the nervous system. It becomes part of you.

At the end of each chapter there's a 'Myths from the Land of You' section, in which readers are invited to find connections between the stories and their own lives. This is a lovely introduction to the idea of myth as a sort of template for human experience.

There are activities and things to do, bringing the stories into practical and playful modes (there's a Songline game and instructions for planting a 'Tun Tree', tracking animals and building a bird box). And there are plenty of riddles.

Georgiana also includes some true-life stories and scientific accounts that connect the story themes with the empirical world.

And the book ends with a challenge – have a story party and tell some of these tales yourself.

The book is life affirming. All of its stories are about taking delight in creation. But there is also a radical undercurrent. Let's not forget what stories do. They are at the root of thought. Narrative psychologists claim that by the age of three we all carry – hard-wired – an internalised narrative grammar. All human modes of conduct (the arts and sciences, memory, planning, religious belief, legislation, craft skills) are deeply storied. Stories are the tools we use to make sense of the world.

They are also viral. They spread. By getting these old stories back into circulation, by encouraging the telling and listening and dispersion of them, and especially by making them available to children, our deep cultural 'story map' can be subtly shifted. They can teach us to reassess our place in creation. Maybe they can lead towards an understanding that sees no contradiction between ancestral knowledge and the concerns of *now*.

It is for this reason most of all that I welcome this book and wish it a happy voyage into the minds and hearts of a new generation of *Natural Storytellers*.

Hugh Lupton, June 2017

Story Sources

For inspired teachers, Forest School leaders, mums, dads, activist uncles, grandmas – and everyone interested in the background and use of these stories.

'The magical understanding by men of the languages of birds and beasts and trees is ... the true purposes of Faerie.'
J R R Tolkien 'On Fairy Stories', 1939.

Where does a story come from? A young Afghan refugee said to me recently, 'Stories don't come from any particular place. They come from the land of Fairytale and Once-upon-a-time.' Stories travel freely across borders without passports.

At the same time it's also true that all the stories in this book came to me from one person in one geographical place. I heard them exactly at that moment. It's an important part of the oral tradition to honour the creation of that storyteller and that place.

Behind the person a fairytale or myth stretches far back into the 'long alchemic processes of time', as Tolkien puts it.

How can we know where a story comes from? Tolkien says:

We must be satisfied with the soup that is set before us, and not desire to see the bones of the ox out of which it has been boiled. By the soup I mean the story as it is served up by its author or teller and by the bones, its sources or material – even when (by rare luck) those can be with certainty discovered.
J R R Tolkien, 'On Fairy Stories', 1939.

Nevertheless, here are a few words about the background, personal and traditional, of these tales ...

Story Heart
Tasoo

This version is from the Quechua Indians of South America. Like all traditional people, the Quechuas have told stories as a way to understand the world, and it's no coincidence that an indigenous people's story is first in this book. Like many such people they have suffered under invaders who took their land and tried to destroy their culture, but storytelling is hard to suppress. For good scholarly accounts of sources, see *Traditional Storytelling Today* edited by Margaret Read MacDonald (Fitzroy Dearborn, 1999).

This story is told in many versions in the Americas and Asia. The Quechua Indians see Tasoo as a hummingbird, a healer or spirit being who helps people in need. After I had written this book I realised that Wangari Maathai told this story too – and I had put her story as the next one!

Wangari and the Green Belt

This is based on the true story of Wangari Maathai and my main source has been *Unbowed* (Anchor, 2007), the autobiography that she wrote about her life. An intense read, often beautifully formulated and without blame. Creating a tale to tell from a 'real life' story is a lot of work and one has to make many choices as to what to include and not. I have also used my imagination to visualise her return to the grandparents' village, for example, though it is not in her book. My method is to work with the story both before and as I tell it. I had the honour to tell Wangari a story in Norway in 2004. I watched her storytelling soul shine out as she listened – it was clear she had a deep understanding of story.

The Pedlar of Swaffham

As a child we had an old '45' vinyl record of Bernard Miles telling this story and we used to listen to it endlessly. When I was eleven my mum took me to Swaffham and we saw the pedlar's statue but there are also versions from Ireland, Scotland, Germany, Austria, Denmark, Turkey, Persia and no doubt many other places. Joseph Jacobs collected this version (*English Fairy Tales*, David Nutt, 1890) and Paolo Coelho has also made his version famous through *The Alchemist* (Harper-Collins, 1993).

Li Chi and Laixi

This is a Chinese story that is pretty popular, probably because it has such a rare 'Heroine slays the dragon' kind of motif. Actually, dragons in Chinese mythology are usually beneficent, so this story has no dragon but a serpent instead. The brave little dog is a feature of the original story but I have given him a bigger part. I have also added his name, a typical Chinese dog's name meaning 'Bringer of Happiness', to give a more positive picture of dogs in China, where they often end up in the soup.

Johnny Appleseed

Johnny was originally called John Chapman – a historical figure from North America, who lived from 1774 to 1845. He has become an important figure in American national mythology. Thanks to Marte Rostvåg for introducing me to Johnny, who has become one of my heroes. Marte has been a big inspiration for this book. She is a biologist and environmentalist who uses stories a lot. She has experimented with eating only locally produced food, both in the autumn and in the spring, which in Norway is no mean feat. Her book about this is *Spis Sørlandet* (Portal, 2013) and she is now an MP for the Green Party.

Story Mind
Brian, Who Was Useless at Storytelling

I first heard Ben Haggarty tell this story in a very different version. Ben and I first told stories together when we were fifteen and he has been a big inspiration (ben-haggarty.com). In Ben's story the hero with no story turns into a woman, gets married, has children, etc. and finally has quite a story to tell. But this version is Irish and I originally found it in the well-loved *Favourite Folk Tales* by Jane Yolen (Pantheon, 1986). I have been told (yes, by an Irish expert) that the Irish have the greatest written collection of traditional stories in the world. Like the Norwegians they have until comparatively recently been a rural society and storytelling remains alive there. I took a group of storytelling students for a study tour to Ireland a few years back and it was moving to hear the pride that so many have in their rich tradition.

The Perfect Pot

The story is said to originate in India. The Indian Vedic tradition is one of the oldest religious sources on the earth and it is primarily oral. So much so that oral sources of the Vedas are often venerated more highly than their written sources. This is in contrast to our 'Religions of the Book' (Christianity, Islam, Judaism) where the written word is more highly valued. Perhaps this makes Indian culture more flexible. With thirty-one official languages and around 880 other languages, India is a huge source of oral traditions. This story was given to me by Marte Rostvåg.

Robin Hood

Robin Hood, the legendary heroic outlaw from the forest who steals from the rich to give to the poor, is lauded in English ballads and tales from the fourteenth century onwards. This kind of hero, who stands up for the common people, is popular in many other cultures, both historical, like William Tell, and in fiction, like Zorro. This story I heard from Benedicte Hambro, a great collector of tales in Norway who works with young people and storytelling. It is also found in her book *Life Is a Banana Tree* by Benedicte Hambro and Hilde Eskild (Ganesa, 2004).

The Rubbish Girl

A classic Norwegian fairytale collected by Asbjørnsen and Moe, who were inspired by the Brothers Grimm in the middle of the nineteenth century. When I started professional storytelling in my early twenties I was fed up with princesses who were pretty prizes, so I did a gender switch. In addition there are several things in the story which children today have no clue about, so this is a classic example of adapting an old tale to one's own time. My contact with these stories is mainly thanks to Marit Jerstad, who has worked with them throughout her life and inspired many Norwegians to see them more deeply (*Fortellerkunst*, Mimir, 2002).

Minding the Way

This story is based on a true story of an Australian Aboriginal woman. Bruce Chatwin coined the word 'songlines' in a book that has been one of my many bibles (*Songlines*, Franklin Press, 1987). He describes the incredible walks Aboriginal peoples have done. As they walk they sing to keep the land alive. Songlines can cover thousands of kilometres.

Aboriginal stories are oral textbooks. The storyteller custodian's role was that of cultural educator. A dreamtime story of ten minutes' length can cover many topics and be suitable for all age groups. The stories contain lessons for children or for bringing renewed understanding to older people. Twenty or more lessons can be found in a single story, teaching about: the spiritual belief system, customs, animal behaviour and psychology, land maps of the region, hunting and gathering skills, cultural norms, moral behaviour, survival skills and food resources.

The Aboriginal community regularly sat under the stars at night around the campfire – and the storyteller's role was to entertain while keeping the culture, history, traditional values and lore of their people alive.

Story Tree

My focus on stories of trees was inspired by my daughter Mari Jerstad, who is a medical herbalist and spent a whole year studying an oak and another year in North Norway painting two birch trees (www.marikaape.no). I also recently discovered a book my dad, Julian Keable, made as a young man with drawings of English trees. The source for this section is perhaps genetic.

Bundle of Sticks

A tale from the famed Aesop. Who this great collector of tales really was is a great story in itself. Some say he was an ugly slave, others a Greek writer of fables, others an Ethiopian collector. His fables have been translated and retold very widely. I changed the gender.

St Peter and the Oak Tree

Folktales about St Peter and the Lord have been fairly common in Scandinavia. St Peter is usually a bit of a comic figure, who can remind one of Hodja. His position as keeper at the pearly gates gives him a role in folktales about attempted entries to heaven. This story is told in Gabriel Scott's book *The Golden Gospel* (originally published in 1921, reissued by Juni, 1998). Maybe Scott was inspired by the old Hodja story in which Hodja is grateful that camels don't have wings so they can't poo on our heads.

All in the Family

Charles Darwin worked for decades on the theory of evolution, but as a Christian he was very unsure whether to make his work public. Then his colleague Alfred Wallace sent him an article about his work in the same area, which prompted Darwin to go ahead and publish. As I was growing up I thought this interpretation of the development of the world was very boring. Then I read The *Secret Life of Trees* by Colin Tudge (Penguin, 2005) and realised how extraordinary it is, as a picture of the deep connection of all life. I began to tell it to teenagers. Every society has their stories, the myths that are the basis of their way of life, and this is one of ours. As time continues, if the stories are told in a boring and uncreative way they will die. They need to be retold for each generation in such a way that they stay fresh and interesting.

The Birch Tree

This appears in a Russian illustrated book given to me by Nina Zelenkova. This exquisite book has no name of either the illustrator or the writer! Several of the tales tell of relation between people and trees.

I have found more stories in non-Western cultures which link us closely with trees, far fewer in Europe. Why? There is quite a lot of evidence that at times the Church has pushed these stories underground. It has been seen as heretical and dangerous to show deep connection with plants and trees. Another Russian friend told me recently that his father was told by an old priest that trees have a soul. This was maintained by many I met on a recent visit to Estonia. The Green Man, carved in many churches throughout the British Isles, is an example of druidic traditions that have lived alongside Christianity.

Hodja

This story was told by Amir Mirzai, a Persian who has made a great contribution to storytelling in Norway. My parents also told us Hodja stories. Hodja is claimed to have been born in Turkey, Afghanistan and Iran. He was an Islamic historic figure of the thirteenth century, but as time has passed many stories have been added of his wisdom and of his foolishness. Many of them are told in a rural settings and have a timeless quality. They can be seen as jokes, but at the same time there is usually a parallel, more subtle aspect. The same stories are told widely further east with heroes of other names and backgrounds.

The Turn Tree

Many years ago, I was touring with the now famous actor from Burkina Faso, Issaka Sawadogo, and he told me a vague outline of such a story. I began to develop and reimagine the story. As I have told the story countless times, it has become a great favorite with children and adults. Years later I asked Issaka about it and he claimed not to remember such a story at all. If ever I meet someone from that part of the world I ask them but, so far, no one has recognised it. In the intervening years many have taken my story and retold it.

Story Animals
The Medicine Bear

There are many Sami stories about bears. The bear was regarded with great reverence in many parts of Sápmi (the area of Sami peoples stretching from Norway eastwards through Sweden, Finland and Russia) and in many places the bear hunt was an important ritual. My daughter Mari Jerstad has a friend – Elise von

Sjeel, a young Sami woman up in Karasjok. She knows Mari has a BA in herbal medicine, so she told her this story. I also have it from a wonderful Finnish book called *Tree People* (Ritva Kovalainen and Sanni Seppo, *Hiilinielu tuotanto and Miellotar*, 1997) given to me by the artist Eva Bakkeslett.

Hodja and Donkey

Another great Hodja story. My Persian friend Amir remembers being told these and many different kinds of stories by a Dervish (a wandering holy man). This man comforted Amir with stories and gave him back a will to live after he had been tortured terribly as a boy. Some sources say Hodja can be found in Persian, Albanian, Armenian, Azerbaijani, Bengali, Bosnian, Bulgarian, Chinese, Greek, Gujarati, Hindi, Judaeo-Spanish, Kurdish, Romanian, Serbian, Russian and Urdu folk traditions. See above ...

The Ark

Climate change made me want to work on this story when I was working with Nina Dessau in Global Migrants for Climate Action. Another inspiration came when I was invited to tell at the large National Storytelling Festival in Iran with Azam Ghasemi. The theme was religious stories and I was the only non-Muslim. The story is found in the Koran but I used the Bible plus a beautiful version by Walter de la Mare. There are versions of Flood stories in the world's oldest written text – *Gilgamesh* – and elsewhere. Archaeological evidence points to them being based on historical events.

Kikko

This story was told by friend Zoe Funge-Smith about her dog Kikko and neighbour Suzy Maynard.

King of the Deer

This story can be found in the *Jataka*, an ancient collection of stories of Buddha's former lives. I was given the book by a great friend, Jon Jerstad. I was helped to develop this version by my daughter Ellen Jerstad, a great storyteller and director (www.ellenjerstad.com). This version is also inspired by Marte Rostvåg, by *Coming Home to Story* by Geoff Mead (Vala, 2011) and a Norwegian version, *Once Buddha Was King of the Monkeys* (Gyldendal, 2003).

Deer Tracker's Game

This is one of several great games I found in Chris Holland's book *I Love My World* (Wholeland Press, 2009).

Story Birds
The Puffin

The ornithological story of the puffin was told to me by Tycho Anker-Nilssen, who has been working with puffins on the islands of Røst faithfully for thirty years. I have connected it to a local legend I heard from Kari Reklev from Kårøy Camping. Kari is a wise and kind woman who was caring for the thousands of kittiwakes nesting on her roofs. Later I heard a very similar story on another island in Lofoten, this time connected not to the loss of birds but to soil erosion. My travels collecting stories in this area can be read on my website and on www.legendhunting.wordpress.com

The Blind Little Sister

I love the way that the two sisters in this story work together. Often in Western fairy tales sisters or brothers are competing against each other. They are jealous and act harshly. But out of Europe this is not always so. I often ask Africans I meet if they have been told stories and, although more and more people are moving into towns, there are still many who have experienced storytelling in their families.

I heard this tale from Hugh Lupton, whom I worked with in the early days of storytelling in the UK. Hugh is one of the best-known storytellers in the land (www.hughlupton.com). He in turn heard it from the famed Scottish storyteller Duncan Williamson, who heard it from a blind man from West Africa in Birmingham. Both Hugh and Duncan have been very important in the renaissance of storytelling in Europe, and both have been most generous in sharing their stories with myself and others. Here again, I have changed the gender of the protagonist.

Francis of Assisi

There are many books about Francis and his life. There is a great Christian tradition of telling stories of the lives of the saints, which has been kept alive mainly in Catholic countries. It is always a big undertaking to retell such a life as that of Francis. Charlotte Øster, my close storytelling collaborator, gave me a children's book on St Francis she had got cheap in a library sale to read on the bus home and I thought, yes, we must use this in our work in the forest. My other main source is from the book my daughter made, age eleven, about the saint, in the Steiner Waldorf tradition where the children don't use printed books but write and draw their own textbook.

Best Friends

This true story from the Second World War is recorded in a gorgeous tiny book, *Sold for a Farthing* by Clare Kipps, published in 1954 (reissued by Peter Smith,

1984). She tells the tale of her relationship with this tiny bird. The title is from the Bible – 'Are not two sparrows sold for a farthing? And one of them shall not fall on the ground without your Father.'

The Hoopoe's Story

The Iranians have a strong storytelling tradition, which I have experienced in Iran. As in most cultures across the world, there have been the professional storytellers, the bards or, as they are called in this region, Ashik, Ashok, or Ashek, and there have been the folk storytellers. This small tale comes from the great Persian epic, *The Conference of the Birds* which would often have been told by a bard with his traditional stringed instrument. I first came across this story as a teenager in the production by Peter Brook.

There is an oral tradition among birds. For example, robins live all their life in a certain territory and pass their own particular song on to their descendants.

The Bashak

Iraq has a rich tradition of storytelling, including the first ever written fiction – *The Epic of Gilgamesh*, written on clay tablets around three thousand years ago. Happily, Gilgamesh seems to be having a revival: I know of several storytellers who tell their own version.

The Bashak is a wonder tale. Again Hugh Lupton lies behind this story, as he recommended a book of Iraqi stories called *Told in the Market Place* (Ernest Benn, 1954).

This theme of bones becoming re-animated is a common one in stories of indigenous peoples.

Story Earth

My brother Rowland Keable was the inspiration for this section. His entire working life has been devoted to earth building, for which he has been awarded a Unesco professorship. Sometimes I tease him, saying he is lucky he has only one story to tell, but he tells it brilliantly.

Ear to the Ground

There is a short film version of this myth in the Sami museum in Karasjok. From discussions I have had in north Norway it seems the story has been largely kept alive among the Swedish Sami people (Harald Gaski – Sami writer and activist). I worked on this tale with Joiker Berit Alette Mienna in a collaboration in which we told in both the Sami and English languages at the Scottish Storytelling Festival.

The Rat Princess

I first heard this story at a festival in Oslo, told by a Danish storyteller, but there are versions from Japan, Iran, India, Korea, North Africa and elsewhere in Europe. Why is it so popular? Maybe because it's comic and at the same time contains a timeless truth. Many Danish folktales are similar to Norwegian and Swedish ones, but this one I have not heard from Norwegian collections. I have developed it with great storyteller Charlotte Øster.

Dirty Earth

The best-known Indian stories are the mighty epics – the *Ramayana* and the *Mahabharata*. Yet like most oral traditions India's spans from those weighty masterpieces to the humble folktale. This story is in honour of Sally Pomme Clayton. Pomme and I met outside the Commonwealth Institute decades ago and I asked her to join the West London Storytelling Unit, where her career as one of the most esteemed tellers began. Sally's version of the story I have retold here is called 'The King with Dirty Feet'. You can find the app of her story on appcrawlr.com/ios/king-with-dirty-feet.

The Story of Earth

As mentioned above, Rowland Keable is my source here; he is constantly finding new ways to tell the story of earth. His entire working life has been focused on renewing this wonderful building material. To do this he has devised ways of telling stories to interest and activate people raised to think that cement is the strongest and best. He has had to think and rethink which narratives can help us understand that cement is a huge emitter and in hot climates often an uncomfortable material to live and work in, requiring air conditioning. This is a new version we collaborated on.

My Land

Afghan culture is steeped in poetry. Taxi drivers or shepherds will often know the great classical poets like Rumi, Hafez and Firdausi and many compose poetry themselves. These poets in turn often use stories within their verses. There has been a rich use of proverbs, legends and folk tales and even amidst a war zone with the struggle for education, especially for girls, there is still an emphasis on stories and poetry in schools. Several Afghans I know can recite large tracts of poetry by heart.

I first heard this story from environmental storyteller Malcolm Green when we gave a course at the Soil Association Conference (www.malcolm-green.co.uk). It's also a Hodja tale.

Roots Make Flowers

This story is found in a book called *The Flowering Tree* by the great collector A K Ramanujan (University of California Press, 1997). These stories are from South India, where the main language is Tamil, and the goddess named is usually in-carnated in South India. My dad was born in Calcutta and India has played an important part in my life. An Indian taxi driver told me on my last visit that every village has their own goddess. She will be unique and different from the goddess in the next village.

Story Water
Salmon Boy

There are many versions of 'Salmon Boy' among First Nations in Canada and the USA. Martin Lee Mueller, who has written a PhD and book entitled *Being Salmon, Being Human* (Chelsea Green, 2017), introduced me to this story. He believes that indigenous stories often carry an empathy with other species that protects biodiversity. I recently realised I also heard this tale years ago from Ben Haggarty.

The Flood

I first heard this story from my dad, Julian Keable, a natural storyteller. It's a Jewish tale but has also wandered a lot. When I think of Jewish storytelling, two things appear. The one is humour and the other is food. Among the many streams of Jewish story is one passed down from grandmother to granddaughter. She is called a 'drut'syla', and Shonaleigh from the UK is one of very few who still keeps this extraordinary oral tradition alive. To get a flavor of Jewish traditional culture I also recommend the book by Isaac Bashevis Singer called *In My Father's Court* (Farrar, Straus and Giroux, 1991).

King Fish in the Sea

This story is found in the Brothers Grimm, the great collectors at the spearhead of the revival of interest in folk literature in Europe. I was recently telling at the Swiss Storytelling Festival, where a splendid German storyteller told me that the

Grimms' tales were forbidden in Germany after the Second World War. This must have been an added loss for the children growing up in that difficult time. The Grimms' stories were told to my family by our mum, Verena Keable, who in turn heard them from her Swiss mother. This is one of the many, many tales she told us as children and was the first story I told in public. It's thanks to her that I became a storyteller. Here I have adapted it into a climate change version, which I have told with the Arctic explorer Tobias Thorleifson.

Living Water

The Tofalars are a tiny group of indigenous people who live in the mountains of Southern Siberia. Before the Russian revolution, they were nomadic, reindeer herders and hunters. They were a peaceful people who were respectful of their children and never hit them. After the revolution young Tofalars went to new Soviet-built schools and were not allowed to speak their mother tongue. Cultural traditions like hunting and shamanism were discouraged or forbidden. The Tofalar are one of the myriad peoples hidden in the mighty Russian empire. I got this story from the internet, which can be a good source.

Dolphin Friends

This is a traditional story from the Yugambeh people, who are Aboriginal Australians from the Gold Coast area. They have been there for 23,000 years! History tells that the immigrant white Australians tried to trick the dolphins by learning the shared language of people and dolphins. Then they slaughtered the dolphins, who never returned. This was such a sad tale I did not include it but there are still people in Brazil who fish with dolphins to this day.

Over the world there are myths, legends and new accounts of dolphins who have saved humans from attacks by sharks or other dangers. But I have a soft spot for sharks. Did you know that in America sharks kill one person every other year, whereas cows kill an average of twenty-two people a year? And by the way, worldwide humans kill well over 100 million sharks every year.

'Dolphin Friends' was developed in discussion with the English woman Amanda Stafford, who has worked to introduce dolphins and other sea mammals to people in a wild setting for over twenty years.

The River

When I was working recently with Norwegian Romani (Gypsy) people in Oslo they told me many stories of their own experiences of storytelling as children. Travelling people often maintain a stronger oral tradition than their sedentary neighbours. It's thanks to them we have retained many tales that would otherwise have been lost. 'The River' comes from a great collection of Romani stories from Sweden, *Det var en gång det som inte var* ('There was once that which was not'), by Bagir Kwiek and Monica Hirsch, Kabusa, 2013). All the stories show a strong relationship with nature.

Story Weather

The idea for this section was inspired by my daughter Dr Heid Jerstad in the Himalayas, where she has done fieldwork on anthropology and climate change (www.weathermatters.net).

The Wind and the Sun

Like 'The Bundle of Sticks', this is known as an Aesop's fable, which I first heard from my mum. A fable is a short wisdom story, often told by oppressed people as a way of expressing what they are forbidden to say openly. As Aesop was reputed to be a slave, he must have understood this well. Recently, when I was collecting tales from Afghans living in Oslo, Mashal Joian told me this as an Afghan story.

Gluscabi and the Wind Eagle

This is an Abenaki First Nation tale that I found years ago in a lovely collection of song stories by the esteemed storyteller Helen East, *The Singing Sack* (A & C Black, 1998). Storytelling is a major part of Abenaki culture as entertainment and teaching method. The Abenaki say stories have lives of their own and are aware of how they are used. If a child behaved badly, rather than being punished, they would be told a story. Joe Bruchac, the great indigenous American storyteller, tells this story beautifully.

Harvesting the Sky

I discovered the Canadians in this story through an article, 'Making Sense of Domestic Warmth' by Phillip Vannini and Jonathan Taggart (in *Body and Society*, 2013). I developed this with the blessing of Professor Phillip Vannini, who has been working with off-gridders for years.

Snow

Again from my Swiss mother Verena Keable and the Brothers Grimm in Germany. The fact that the girls go to the underworld is linked to the original name of the story – 'Frau Holle'. This again connects with Hel (Hell), a character from the underworld in Norse mythology. This story type is said to be the most well-known story pattern in the world. There is an international categorisation system called the Aarne–Thompson tale types, which lists it as type 480. There is a whole book devoted to these stories called *The Kind and Unkind Girls* by Warren E Roberts (Wayne State University Press, 1994), where one can study many versions, including, for example, twelve from Latvia, though it was subsequently discovered there are actually 109 Latvian versions in print! The Russian folklorist Vladimir Propp was also inspired by this particular story to look at the structure of the classic *Russian Fairy Tales* collected by Afanas'ev (Pantheon, 1976).

Rain Magic, Sun Magic, Wind Magic

The source of these stories is *The Golden Bough* by James George Frazer (online edition available). This monumental study in comparative folklore, magic and religion shows parallels between rites, beliefs, superstitions and taboos of early cultures and Christianity. It goes into all sorts of fascinating areas like the relics of tree worship, killing the divine animal, and public scapegoats. When published in 1922 it had a great impact on psychology and literature and remains an early classic anthropological resource.

Rain

This story was collected by the great Hugh Tracey. After the First World War his brother was given land in Zimbabwe and Hugh came to help him on the farm. He came from Yorkshire and was very fond of singing. As he worked he sang with the other farm workers and discovered a wealth of music, until then given little or no respect by Western culture. His was an important impetus to honour the music and stories of the Shona people. Every story contains a song.

The First Party

This story from the Inuit in Greenland I got from Marte Rostvåg. It was collected by the Danish/Greenland Polar explorer Knud Rasmussen, born in 1879. His father was a missionary but his mother was local and Knud grew up in Greenland, spoke Inuit and as a boy learnt to hunt, paddle a kayak and drive a dog-sleigh. He heard the story by the Coleville river.

Using the Story

A story speaks for itself and will be much smaller if we limit it to one meaning. P L Travers, creator of Mary Poppins, once told me that a story is like a crystal; hold it up to the light and all the colours of the rainbow will shine through it. Here are a few tips about how I have used stories. Your only limit is your imagination.

Story Heart
The Story of Tasoo

This story has been a favourite among environmentalists and activists – however small you are it's worth doing what you can. It's a great tale because it's so simple. When starting to learn storytelling it's important for most apprentices to have a solid simple structure. That makes it easy to hold in the mind and to add your own images and twists when you so wish.

Wangari and the Green Belt

I use this story during a day in the forest with twelve-year-olds. The day is an adventure where they learn about species, test themselves and hear many tales. We walk barefoot and it's very interesting how differently they behave after this particular story. Before the story they can be quite hysterical if they see an ant and express lots of drama about how painful it is on their feet, but after this story the atmosphere changes and a different perspective emerges. Many don't want to put their shoes back on. We conclude the day by giving them a small tree to plant.

I have also told this story for adults but then I have reworked it so that it is more nuanced and complex. When working with adults timing needs to be more precise.

Tolkien was convinced that fairytales are primarily for adults. I don't agree, I think they are for everyone but I'm sure that some adult readers will wish to use stories from the book for adult audiences too.

The Pedlar of Swaffham

A versatile story. I have used it as a pilgrimage story, as I walk a lot with adults and children on the Pilgrim's Way that goes outside my door. Telling stories outside in tandem with being active and experiencing the forest can be a powerful way to work. But it is important to be secure in the story and in the walking or other activities you are doing outdoors. It may look easy but requires years of preparation of one kind and another!

Most traditional cultures have many stories about dreams and relied on dreaming for guidance at times. This story can also be useful as an introduction to work with our own dreams and stories.

Li Chi and Laixi

A simple story, fairly easy to tell and good to lift the courage of girls. It's also interesting as part of a huge genre of people killing monsters. George Monbiot's book *Feral* (University of Chicago Press, 2017) talks about rewilding, how humans have been causing extinction for millennia and the need for predators. This story can be an opening for discussion about predators and their vital place in biodiversity. (See also 'Salmon Boy'.)

Johnny Appleseed

Good to tell when you are working with seeds and planting trees. Johnny was vegetarian and anti-racist at a time when you rarely hear of such things.

In our outdoor projects we like to include local pensioners. Usually we un-earth people with lots of resources who have much to share with children and teenagers. Often they are shy at first, but after a little experience some transform fast so that their language and themes fit an enthusiastic young audience.

Story Mind

Brian, Who Was Useless at Storytelling

Stories about storytelling are always useful. When you are giving a course or arranging an evening of stories, it's good to have a story about how hopelessly bad someone was at telling stories until ... This is a story about attitude: Brian thought he had no talents, but actually was full of them.

The Perfect Pot

Perfect story to discuss recycling. The great thing about stories is you can tell them without moralising. Moralising tends to have the opposite of the desired effect. I have had a lot of fun holding workshops on storytelling and recycling. We sit and remake or mend something as we practise and listen to stories. Using your hands develops the mind and creativity. This story is good as part of an art or craft course.

Robin Hood

Useful for storytelling workshops. This story illustrates how stories can be used

TH E NATURAL STORYTELLER

in very different situations. Ashley Ramsden, storytelling mentor, once said to me, 'You only really need one story. Just keep telling it in different ways.'

I also used this story on a course I held on storytelling and archery. The course was held in the forest in Norway; we all made a bow and began to learn to shoot while at the same time working on stories about archers.

The Rubbish Girl

Again a great recycling story. It is also a story with a lovely unpretentious female protagonist.

Minding the Way

This story can be told to introduce the songlines exercise at the end of *Story Mind*. Or with any kind of walk you are planning to do — especially a night walk, usually very popular with kids. I have worked a lot with walking and storytelling. It's perfect to tell a story and then walk together, giving time for digestion and discussion. Discussion side by side can happen in a more relaxed way than face to face.

Story Tree
The Bundle of Sticks

Useful for squabbling children but also at adult conferences! I am asked on a regular basis to tell stories at conferences, often on environmental or cultural themes. It's a very interesting experience time and again, that the atmosphere and quality of attention changes as the story begins. It's clear to me that we are using a different part of the brain when we listen to a story; in fact we are using more of the right brain in addition to the left brain. This makes stories much more likely to be remembered than facts, figures and discussion.

St Peter and the Oak Tree

If you are working with this story it can be fun to really go to town on the many uses of an oak tree. It can either be told from the mouth of the Lord, or of the storyteller. Do some research on carpentry and carving of oak, with all the animals and birds including ourselves that have enjoyed its protein-rich acorns, and on the uses of its bark and roots. Wonderful if you can also extend into meeting such a tree, in spring with its tiny red female flowers and showy male catkin flowers, or perhaps in autumn when you might want to try eating the acorns or soaking and cooking them, perhaps roasting them for coffee.

This is also a story about how we humans can't afford to play around with nature or there may be worse side-effects than we can even imagine. In the age of gene technology this is an important story.

All in the Family

I use this story in a programme for thirteen/fourteen-year-olds, which takes place in the house of the explorer Thor Heyerdahl in South Norway. I am in role as Thor's rather fierce mother, a great fan of Darwin who regarded religion as old fashioned, while his father would secretly pray with him before bed-time. Talking about science in this kind of context works very well; the teenagers are very engaged and although the first thing I say is, 'I moved into this house almost 100 years ago ...' there are always one or two of them who ask if I am really Thor Heyerdahl's mother.

The Birch Tree

We have told this story on botanical projects in the forest. Birds in captivity is also a central theme in this story, as is our connection with other species in general. Dr Martin Lee Mueller, who I collaborate with in *The Salmon Fairy Tale* is convinced that a key function of stories is to connect us to other species. As soon as we identify with a hawk or a salmon in a story we understand it as a living being on a par with ourselves. As I have worked on the stories of salmon my attitude has altered dramatically. I used not to care about fish at all. Now I find myself sitting on the bus imagining I am a fish, and experience the salmon factories as an unworthy and terrible industry.

Hodja

Hodja is a wonderful ambassador for the Islamic world. He is so unpretentious and warm. Here he is a total environmentalist. This little tale can be used to explore different species and investigate botany. Which tree should he plant? How old is a tree before it bears fruit? The story can be combined with an expedition to collect seeds and nuts and then try to germinate them. As with all such projects there needs to be much good preparation both practically and in terms of knowledge. I have spent much time learning botany for storytelling projects, but have found it double fun. Really fun to learn it and then really fun to share the knowledge.

The Tun Tree

This story is popular in our project for schools – 'The Voice of the Forest'. I am in role as a contemporary of Darwin, botanist Marianne North. I wear a bonnet and black Victorian dress complete with hooped skirt. As well as telling stories of trees, I ask groups of eleven and twelve-year-olds to help me to identify the local trees, as I am shortly going to be reporting to the Royal Geographical Society in London. They throw themselves wholeheartedly into this task. I then say that I would like them to see each tree as an individual not just a species and proceed with an exercise that often ends with boys spontaneously hugging 'their' tree.

With its message of the extraordinary generosity of nature this is one of my all-time favourites.

Story Animals
The Medicine Bear

Perfect for introducing herbs and the uses of botanical plants and trees in both medicine and countless other areas. Mari Jerstad, Charlotte Øster and I have devised a programme for nine-year-olds in which they learn about four different ordinary 'weeds' and their medical properties. This story is included, plus a tea ceremony, games and stories from historical people working in this area.

Hodja and Donkey

Death is a big theme in stories, perhaps because it's often hard for adults to face in daily life. I love this story for its absurdity and its extra layer – after all, what better than making a temple to your dear donkey?

The Ark

A story that can be used in discussion of climate change and continuing the theme of courage and inter-species responsibility. When I told this story in Iran, we used dual language storytelling. This is a technique we have developed over the years since my first visit there in 2006. We have used it with many languages – examples are available on my website www.georgiana.net and on www.morsmal.no. Telling religious stories has its own challenge – how to make it non-dogmatic? In my opinion a true prophet does not preach but tells a good story with no strings attached. One great aspect with this story is that versions are found in all the Religions of the Book.

Kikko

How to use stories from everyday life? This can be the starting point for sharing our own stories of pets or wild animals we have met. This theme is pretty much guaranteed to elicit tales from most children.

King of the Deer

This is a big story – not one to start with as a new storyteller but one with the mightiest message. Remember, as the great storyteller Jan Blake once told me, when you are telling a myth or a big story don't tell it in a stiff pompous way. Don't let your body go rigid and announce, 'This story is very important.' Rather enter it as a human, with humour, and take us on the journey. Told well, this story is a good ambassador for reducing meat-eating.

Story Birds
The Puffin

In 2015 puffins joined the endangered species list, so this is, sadly, a more relevant story now than ever. Seabirds also act as an indicator for the life of the oceans; they are dependent on the life in the sea.

The Blind Little Sister

This is a story of so-called disabilities that are turned into strengths. It can be used as part of an exploration of the senses. I have worked on this with teenagers, beginning with a discussion of which sense they would least like to lose. Then we divided into two groups, one blindfolded and the other with ear-plugs.

We were out at a cabin in the mountain and for two hours we became 'blinded' or 'hearing impaired'. Those with the ear plugs kept an eye on those with blind folds. Then we swapped roles for a further two hours. A powerful sensory experience, at the end of which some people did not want to remove the blind-fold, they had entered such a deep listening.

Francis of Assisi

St Francis has been named the saint of ecology. All truly holy people must surely share a realisation that humans are part of a greater creation, and Francis is a brilliant example. He also shares with Hodja a sense of fun and of going beyond ordinary morality. For some of the children I tell stories to, who are financially well off, it's easy to identify with this rich kid who became a humble servant of creation.

Best Friends

Good starting point for discussion of our relationships with other species.

The Hoopoe's story

A story that lends itself to discussion. Why not use a method called 'Socratic Dialogue'? The guidelines are simple. A statement is made – for example 'Stories are boring', 'Looking beautiful is important' or 'The smallest are the weakest'. Take a minute for everyone to think about the statement. Do they agree or disagree? Those who wish to give their view raise their hand. Whoever made the statement picks a speaker. The speaker says if they agree or disagree with the statement and then says why. Encourage them to give an example of why they think like this. No one is allowed to interrupt. When they are finished others may raise their hand and they choose the next speaker. In this way no one is forced to directly interpret the story. The story is simply told as a window to pondering.

The Bashak

Station teaching can work very well after a story. I used this story in a programme about Islamic art with children from six to eight years. I developed aspects of the story to describe art and craft. The boy's mother wove beautiful carpets, and I went into great detail about the architecture and art of the king's palace. After they have listened to the story, which takes about thirty-five minutes to tell, the children have a choice of activities. Some play with Islamic-inspired costumes. Some listen to Islamic music in a specially designed small palace with mirror mosaic. The third group draw a tiny picture inspired by the story. Here I encourage them to take the Islamic model, drawing and decorating everything except humans. Then they swap so by the end they have taken part in all the activities. It is a chance to really dive into this world of the wonder tale and also to cherish and value the rich culture of Iraq and the Middle East.

Story Earth
Ear to the ground

Sharing this creation story I sometimes ask the children to listen to the ground. What is it saying?

The Rat Princess

This story works well for younger children. For seven years I had my own nursery school where we told stories every day. Usually we told the same story Monday to Friday. Adults are often frightened of repetition; children love it, and can understand so much more deeply one story heard many times. As the week proceeded often the children would want to start playing the story and we might give them a few props to facilitate this.

It's also fun to use this story as a model to make up a circular story. After it's been told a few times together we can develop our own version. At this age a child won't usually do this alone but may with prompting from an adult: 'There was once a ... who wanted to get the best present in the world for its child. So it got a ... But then it met ... Who said, "Ah, that's not the best present because ... The best present is ..."' And so on.

Dirty Earth

In my version there is also a song where the audience joins in the actions. The first time we sing to encourage the raja to wash. Every time Satish Satash has to clean up the earth the audience helps him by repeating the same melody with simple words and the actions of sweeping, washing then sewing. As part of a storytelling hour I often have one story with participation.

The Story of Earth

The discussion of climate change is pretty new. Here is another way to open up the story for the new generation.

My Land

Capitalism and land ownership in a nutshell! Stories can make a very good contribution to a conference. Within moments one senses that a different part of the brain comes into use.

Roots Make Flowers

A story rich with themes. In Sweden a decade back there was a secondary school that tried a daring experiment. They began the term with only one thing on the curriculum – a story. From the questions this story brought came all the activities and studies of that term. As the term approached its end, the teacher reported looking at all the activities and crossing off Maths, Geography, History, Physics, Swedish, English, etc. Everything had emerged from the interest of the pupils. This story might be such a starting point.

Story Water
Salmon Boy

Like the true story of wolves being re-introduced to Yellowstone Park, or the importance of sea otters, this is a key story about biodiversity. We use it as part of a programme about wild salmon and farmed salmon. The Norwegian fish industry is currently polluting most of our fresh water and destroying the habitats of wild salmon in what they ironically have branded 'The Salmon Fairytale'. Storytelling as a full evening performance can work brilliantly for adults. We have an adult performance of the same name with Joiker Torgeir Vassvik and Dr Martin Lee Mueller. See www.georgiana.net

The Salmon Boy story is a tale of transformation. If we use the imagination and think about becoming animal, insect or bird, we may empathise with other species than our own.

The Flood

Climate change and a picture that perhaps all the available technology to save us is already in place; we just need to see that.

King Fish in the Sea

This version is focused on climate change and consumerism. It's an old story – it can be comforting to know that people have always had a problem with greed!

Living Water

This can be used as a starting point for a discussion on bullying, cultural diversity, eternal life. Instead of immediately discussing the intellectual themes of a story it is usually best to work artistically with it first. Tools given in this book and many others can explore the story imaginatively before one begins to open up the themes and ideas lying behind it.

Dolphin Friends

A story showing how different species can work together. In telling a story from a traditional culture far from our own it is important to try and research as best one can. The absolutely best way to do this is by meeting with a living bearer of that culture, but that isn't always an easy thing to do.

    The pace of change means that even elders of our own culture from a generation or two back have so many experiences that are very exotic to children growing up today. When working with children and a story it can be very enriching to meet elders from their local community. And of course the older generation are usually delighted to be heard.

The River

I tell this story with two musicians, one a Norwegian accordion player who has devoted her life to Gypsy music and one a large Romanian Gypsy to be found playing his saxophone on the street even in the freezing snow. It's such a luxury to tell with musicians and can lift a story immensely. However it's a mistake to believe it is easy. It may just fall into place but that depends on the listening of both parties and usually needs proper rehearsal.

Story Weather
The Wind and the Sun

A nice short story to start with. When you are putting together a programme of different stories it can often work well to have a short story to open with. An icebreaker that helps you begin to know your audience and vice versa.

Gluscabi and the Wind Eagle

A great favourite with younger children. A story with a song, I use this as a participation story. You might find your own melody for the text or go to *The Singing Sack* by Helen East and use the tune there.

Harvesting the Sky

When you come across something that inspires you, what better than to develop and retell a story about it? It may travel the world bringing ideas and practices with it.

Snow

It can be transformative to tell a story to one particular child. When I had my nursery school there was one child who really annoyed me. She always went round disturbing other children's activities. Suddenly I realised what she was doing. She was trying to help them. So I told her this story about helping. A small miracle happened and our whole relationship was changed. A link was made and feelings of irritation transformed into love. She grew up to become a nurse.

Rain, Sun and Wind Magic

These stories may help us to make our own rituals in nature. Children often like to make rituals but they need to be presented in a non-pretentious way. They can lead to a deeper appreciation of the natural world. Often one can begin with a wonder tale (a longer story with a magical element) and then move into a shared activity where a feeling of reverence emerges. The activity must be prepared carefully beforehand so that the whole focus can be on being there. On the other hand sometimes a ritual may emerge spontaneously.

Rain

I have used this story in a performance with Raymond and Kouame Sereba from Ivory Coast. We used it to discuss the place of the immigrant or stranger. In their language the word for 'stranger' is the same as the word for 'guest'. In a medieval form of Latin the word for 'stranger' is the same as the word for 'wolf'. And we know that our attitudes to the wolf have destroyed them in most European countries.

The story can also be told to open our relation to weather. Most of us in Europe complain about rain, but it may be life or death for farmers further South.

The Last Story

What better tale for any celebration or story party?

About the Author

Georgiana has been a pioneer for the rebirth of storytelling in Norway and England. Legend-hunting, she tracks down stories reflecting our relationship with nature. She launched the Norwegian Storytelling festival in 2004 and has been teaching storytelling at Oslo University since 1997. In 2002 Georgiana founded *Fortellerhuset* with tellers from three continents and has led work with dual language stories since 2006.

Georgiana puts on her tattered cloak and walks outside her door on Oslo's east side onto the Pilgrims' Way with hundreds of teenagers each year. During the walk, they get attacked by bandits, pass by ancient sites from pre-Christian times, walk barefoot and then the final trial – they walk in silence. Mainly from immigrant backgrounds, as if entering a fairytale, they engage intensely with nature and story.

A second annual adventure is based on the Norwegian adventurer, Thor Heyerdahl. Fifty fourteen-year-olds cycle to the house where the great man grew up. Here Georgiana tells how as a child he was not allowed to play with other children. He was very shy and hopeless at school but loved being outside. By the age of thirty, floating over the huge Pacific Ocean on a raft, he had still not learnt to swim. So this man, who is a household name accross the whole world, started out like a bit of a loser. The teenagers realise that you don't have to be a classic hero to achieve great things. Then they go into role as 'climate witnesses' from across the globe. They identify with these people and together find solutions.

(At the end Georgiana says, 'When Thor Heyerdahl was an old man they said: "Thor, did you ever find Paradise, which you were searching for your whole life?" And he answered, "I have travelled over the seven seas, I have met kings and presidents, princesses and movie stars, but one thing I can promise you. To find paradise you don't need to leave the Larvik Fjord. Because to find paradise, you must search into your own heart."')

In the role of nineteenth-century botanist Marianne North, Georgiana tells in the forest to over one thousand teenagers every year at the site of the Viking ship burial in south Norway. Themes of life and death, wealth and satisfaction combine with the story of an 800-year-old oak tree and many stories told in this book. At the end of the journey they can recognise most of the local species and have won a baby tree to plant and care for.

In her project 'Legend-hunting', she walked for seven weeks, sleeping in a hammock by night and by day collecting stories from strangers about how people and nature are connected.

She has told at festivals in Norway, Denmark, Sweden, Finland, England, Scotland, Switzerland, Estonia, India and Iran, travelling overland or by sea as much as possible. Georgiana recently received the Oslo City Art Award for outstanding contribution to the cultural life of Oslo.

www.georgiana.net

 Georgiana Keable The Story of Nature and the Nature of Story

Other Books in the Storytelling Series from Hawthorn Press

An A-Z Collection of Behaviour Tales
From Angry Ant to Zestless Zebra
Susan Perrow
Foreword by Georgiana Keable

Susan offers story medicine as a creative strategy to help children age 3-9 years face challenges and change behaviour. Following the alphabet, each undesirable behaviour is identified in the story title: anxious, bullying, demanding, fussy, jealous, loud, obnoxious, uncooperative, and more. The stories, some humorous and some serious, are ideal for parenting, teaching and counselling.
978-1-907359-86-6; 234 x 156mm; 144pp

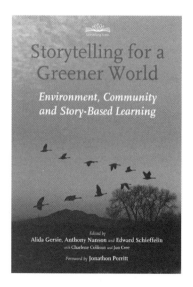

Storytelling for a Greener World
Environment, Community and
Story-Based Learning
Alida Gersie, Anthony Nanson and Edward Schieffelin, with Charlene Collison and Jon Cree

The what, why and how of storytelling and storywork to promote environmental mindfulness and sustainable behaviour in adults and children. Written by 21 cutting-edge professionals, the book includes over 40 stories, many creative activities and detailed descriptions of inspiring practice for organisations, NGOs, schools, colleges and communities.
978-1-907359-35-4; 234 x 156mm; 368pp

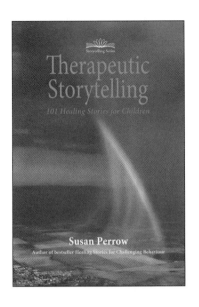

Therapeutic Storytelling

Susan Perrow

Foreword by Jennifer Gidley PhD

This treasury of 101 new healing stories addresses a range of issues – from unruly behaviour to grieving, anxiety, lack of confidence, bullying, teasing, nightmares, intolerance, bedwetting and much more.

978-1-907359-15-6; 234 × 159mm; 272pp

The Storyteller's Way

A sourcebook for inspired storytelling

Sue Hollingsworth, Ashley Ramsden

To tell a story well you need a certain set of skills, and this book is an essential guide. It contains a wealth of stories, exercises, tips and insights to guide your storytelling path, offering time-tested and trusted ways to improve your skills, overcome blocks and become a confident and inspirational storyteller. Use *The Storyteller's Way* to tell stories for entertainment, teaching, coaching, healing or making meaning.

978-1-907359-19-4; 228 × 186mm; 256pp

Ordering Books

If you have difficulties ordering Hawthorn Press books from a bookshop, you can order direct from our website **www.hawthornpress.com** or the following distributors:

UNITED KINGDOM
BookSource
50 Cambuslang Road,
Glasgow, G32 8NB
Tel: (0845) 370 0063, Email: orders@booksource.net

USA/NORTH AMERICA
Steiner Books
PO Box 960, Herndon, VA 20172-0960, USA
Tel: (800) 856 8664, Email: service@steinerbooks.org
www.steinerbooks.org

Waldorf Books
Phil & Angela's Company, Inc.
1271 NE Hwy 99W #196, McMinnville, Oregon 97128, USA
Tel: (503) 472-4610, Email: info@waldorfbooks.com
www.waldorfbooks.com

AUSTRALIA & NEW ZEALAND
Footprint Books Pty Ltd 4 /8 Jubilee Avenue,
Warriewood, NSW 2102, Australia
Tel: (02) 9997 3973, Email: info@footprint.com.au
www.footprint.com.au

Hawthorn Press